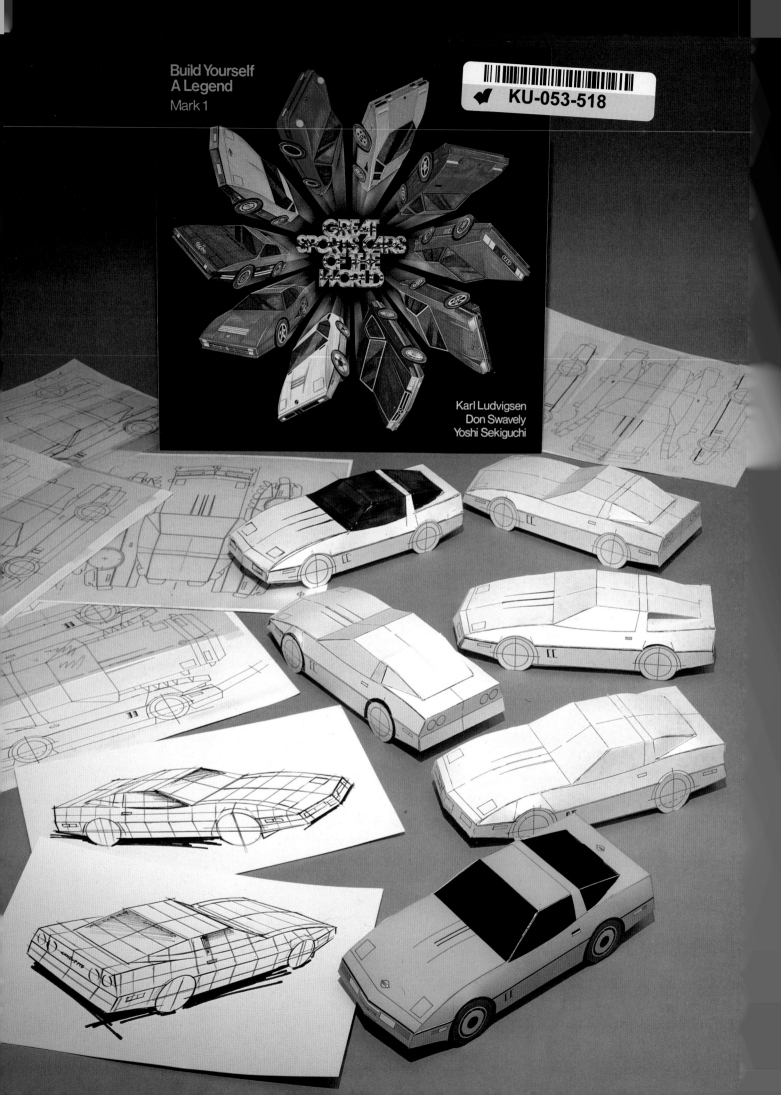

Build Yourself
A Legend

Mark 1

GREAT
SPORTS CARS
OF THE
WORLD

Karl Ludvigsen
Don Swavely
Yoshi Sekiguchi

ABOUT THIS BOOK

DEDICATION AND ACKNOWLEDGEMENT

This book is a very personal, behind the scenes look at visual communications through my experiences. It's about failures and successes, accepted and rejected works, how concepts were developed, and how I handled clients.

A number of books have been published about graphic design, but most of them are by famous and popular designers for the main purpose of glorifying their works. Many of the authors of these books have worked for giant corporations with huge budgets.

INSIDE DESIGN focuses not only on samples of accepted design solutions, but on many superior designs that were rejected and never before seen by the public. It also takes a realistic look at the design process from concept development to the finished product.

When I present my design solutions to a client, I make it a rule to submit three designs, each derived from a different approach. It is important to involve the client in the selection process. However, too often a client chooses the design that is not the best in terms of pure graphic design. Design should be functional and not executed only for design's sake, but the truth is, many of the most creative and inspirational designs are filed away and forgotten. Therefore, I thought it important that this book should include examples of both success and rejection.

It is a privilege to work with my friend, Mort Goldsholl, on this book. Curious about many things, Goldsholl does not confine himself to a narrow, specific field but covers a broad area of both design and film. With Goldsholl's expertise in packaging, exhibits, corporate communications, film and product design, and my experience with advertising, promotion, still photography, publication design and illustration, INSIDE DESIGN covers nearly all aspects of design activity in the U.S. today.

When I presented the concept for this book to Graphic-sha Publishing Company of Tokyo, we had tentatively named the book "1 + 1," emphasizing the combination of works of two designers, one American, the other Japanese. It was then changed to "Beyond Design" because it was thought that the original title, though appropriate, needed additional explanation. Our second choice meant that the book dealt with more than just accepted design solutions. Finally, we agreed on "INSIDE DESIGN" because it best describes what this book is all about — the sweat, tears and personal satisfaction of our careers.

I think it is important that you know how and why this book came about. It is also important that you know more about me to better understand my approach to specific design problems. That is why I have included a short synopsis of my life among the pages of this book. You will notice a small part of me in every design that I have created.

I asked Mort Goldsholl to participate in this project because I respect him as a great designer and film maker, but above all, because I love him as a truly sincere and warm person. The logic for sharing this book is simple — East and West have finally met through the eyes and minds of two very different designers. I hope you find it interesting.

Three Years From Concept To Finish
(Picture on previous page)

Everyone must have constructed a model from cut-out paper patterns at least once. A concept was born three years ago using this idea to make car models for advertising and publication. After making numerous patterns and models, with much trial and error, I succeeded in making perfect models without using glue. It is similar to Japanese Origami.
(Story on page 17)

This book is dedicated to my wife, Yoshiko, for following my sometimes difficult path of life and work for the past 27 years without a complaint and for giving me the most wonderful gifts of life, my three daughters.

I would also like to acknowledge the other people who have helped me realize this dream:

My clients and friends who made this book possible.

Mort and Millie Goldsholl, who understood the meaning of publishing this book and gave me their full support in assembling pages as well as in my private life.

Nao and Yokko Hisai, who collected toys from my childhood and memorabilia from my singing career.

My second daughter, Chika, who coordinated the very difficult task of production of this book.

Colette Urban, who rewrote and edited copy so that my English would make sense.

Satoru Fujii, who introduced me to Graphic-sha Publishing Company of Japan.

Toshiro Kuze, publisher, for his foresight and courage to put this out into the world.

Rico Samejima, who did a wonderful job of coordinating this project and Nobuhiko Yamada, a very capable editor, who did so much in completing this book.

Larry Nordal of Vision Art, who supplied the art of typesetting.

Merle Haggard, whose country music tapes kept me company while working late nights and early mornings on many occasions. "Big City" is playing right now:

> *"Been working every day
> since I was twenty,
> Haven't got a thing to show
> for anything I've done..."*

I am glad to say, I now have something to show.

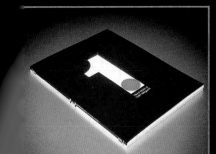

INSIDE DESIGN
WHERE A CONCEPT UNFOLDS

SEKIGUCHI

CONTENTS

INSIDE DESIGN
WHERE A CONCEPT UNFOLDS
by Yoshi Sekiguchi
Copyright © 1987
by Graphic-sha Publishing Co., Ltd.

ISBN 4-7661-0417-X
Printed in Japan
First edition April 1987
Graphic-sha Publishing Co., Ltd.
1-9-12, Kudan-Kita, Chiyoda-ku
Tokyo 102, Japan
Telephone (03) 263-4318
Facsimile (03) 263-5297
Telex J29877 GRAPHIC

CHILDHOOD DREAM (1931–1945)

There is a legend in the Sekiguchi family. One day, the youngest son, two-year-old Yoshinobu, heard the fairy tale, "Urashima Taro." Yoshinobu asked his mother where the dragon castle in the fairy tale could be found:

"It is in the clear sea, Bo-oya (small boy)."

"Then he went into the water riding a turtle?"

"Yes..."

"How was he able to breathe?"

His mother was unable to find a logical answer.

"Oh, then it must be a fairy tale," the son concluded.

I do not remember this incident as it happened, but heard it told repeatedly by my mother to neighbors and friends over cups of green tea. I clearly remember her expression as she told this story. Her eyes would get very narrow and there was a hint of a smile in her cheeks. She must have been very proud of me.

I had three brothers and two sisters, all of them older than me. My favorite pastime was to stick around them while they were studying or reading books. By the time I started grammar school, I was reading third grade books. When I look back now, I sometimes think I must have been a little brat, like a grown man in a boy's body.

My favorite class was arts and crafts. I was superior! So superior that when the school submitted my works to national competitions, the judges would not believe that they were

done by me so I was eliminated from entering. Again, I think that perhaps my paintings were too adult-like, lacking the wonderful, childish, fanciful qualities of the other children's work.

The games that we played in that era bring back many happy childhood memories. Playing soldiers was one of my most cherished pastimes. As soon as we returned home from school, all the boys would get together armed with bamboo sticks for swords and rifles. We would run through fields and over hills trying to defeat one another. We also used to play Menko. A Menko is similar to a baseball card with pictures of Sumarai warriors and Sumo wrestlers. We would try to flip our opponent's Menko card upside down by slapping them against each other.

Local events would always draw a crowd. Once a month was "En-nichi" night, when street vendors would gather around the local shrine. Toys lit by bare bulbs strung between the trees were visible up and down the streets. I can still visualize and feel the excitement of those nights, but the most entertaining thing among all of the events I experienced as a child was "Kami-shibai" (paper drama). Realistic pictures painted in full color were placed in a shallow box with a face cut out. It was as if a TV screen was removed and a stack of pictures on thick cardboard was in its place. While telling a story, the player would change the scene one by one. The box would

be placed on a bicycle rack, turning the street corner into an instant theatre. The player would come out in the late afternoon and clap two sticks of wood together announcing his arrival. Within minutes, he was surrounded by an audience of young boys.

Other fond childhood memories include browsing through the illustrated books from Koudansha. These books were expensive so friends and neighbors would buy different editions and exchange with one another. Popular cartoons, such as "Norakuro," "Adventurous Dankichi," "Tank Tankuro," and "Fuku-chan" were among my favorites.

The city where I was born, Yokosuka, had the largest harbor and ship-building facilities in Japan as well as the Imperial Navy headquarters. Almost everyone was connected to the Navy in one way or another. All of the boys planned to be in the Navy and all the girls dreamed of marrying Navy officers.

One cold December morning, the radio announcer told of the Pacific War. I was excited at the time that we could finally smash the ABCD (America, Britain, China and Dutch) surrounding ring.

My father was a navy officer and my three brothers were all pilots, so naturally I too was determined to be a fighter pilot, preferably flying Zeros. The art I constructed then reflected the era. I painted pictures of air battles, built many model airplanes and, as a result, neglected my studies.

The painter I loved the most was Katsuichi Kabashima, who painted every cover of "Kouku Shonen" or Boys Aviation, published by Seibundo Shinkosha. His paintings were so realistic that they looked like color photographs (which didn't even exist at the time).

After the sea battle of Midway, the tide of the war turned against Japan. Many schools closed for fear of air raids, many of my friends left to live in the countryside and those who stayed were drafted to do light labor for the Navy. One of my friends and I were assigned to take care of two sheep in an oil storage station for the Navy. We took the sheep up to the top of a hill from where Oppama Navy airfield was clearly visible. It was like heaven for a boy who loved airplanes since I could watch top secret planes being tested. I painted images of these planes in my memory and made sketches on paper when I returned home. I sent some of these drawings to my friend who had left the city.

Then something very frightening occurred. I was summoned by the infamous Kenpeitai (army police troop), known for torturing people and making them confess. During the war, all letters that went out of the city were inspected to protect military secrets. They had gotten a hold of the letters and drawings of the airplanes that I had sent my friend and thought that I was a spy reporting on their airplanes to the enemy. My father and three brothers had

gone to war so my eldest sister, Toshiko, escorted me. She was a teenager at the time and must have been as scared as I was.

As soon as I entered the room, I saw all of my letters and drawings heaped in a pile on the desk. A lieutenant saw me and said, "This little kid did this?!" When they realized that I was not an adult (which they had assumed by seeing the sketches), they knew that a mistake had been made.

The last year of the war was the worst of times. We heard the news that Kamikaze special attack forces were formed. I did not feel sympathy for those pilots taking off for almost certain death, but rather found them courageous and heroic. I would do the same when the time arrived, I thought. It wasn't until two months after the war had ended that we learned that my two brothers had crashed to their deaths as Kamikaze pilots.

August 11, 1945 was a very hot day with no clouds in the blue sky. I was on the beach when a B-29 dropped a leaflet announcing that a new type of bomb had been droppped in Hiroshima and that Japan had accepted an unconditional surrender. I was somewhat disappointed that my dream of becoming a fighter pilot would not be realized.

At noon on August 15, the Emperor addressed the Japanese people by radio to announce the end of the war. Even so, young pilots flew over

our city to show their intention of continuing the fight and anti-aircraft guns were still active against American planes for several days.

The dust finally settled and Americans came to Yokosuka on September 2. My father was at the Navy headquarters at the time. He had been assigned to lower the chrysanthemum, the sign for the royal family, from the main building. His interpreter, Tatsuo Shibata, was a Japanese sailor born in the State of Washington. Shibata became an editor-in-chief for the Mainichi (a newspaper in English), and would later help me personally.

I was 14 years old, and a second grader in junior high, when faced with a tragedy of defeat that Japan had never before experienced. Now we had to welcome the Americans, whom we had called Kichiku (devilish animal), to the sacred Navy city of Yokosuka.

AMERICANIZATION (1945–1964)

Never before in the history of mankind, I believe, has a conquered nation welcomed so eagerly the occupation forces without a trace of resistance. Within a matter of days, Japanese people went from praising and thanking the military rule to condemning it for the evils it had perpetrated. Seemingly overnight American democracy was in place. Before the occupation, the order of classes was Samurai (warrior), farmer, manufacturer, merchant. This was completely reversed to merchant, manufacturer, farmer, Samurai.

Since our city had wholly supported the Japanese Navy, most of the families had suffered losses. It might have been the military rulers who started the war and lost, but common people, like my father, brothers and all the others who fought for the sake of the country, dedicated their lives. They should not be held responsible at all. Our family lost two boys, and my father and other brother were forbidden to work for a long time. It must have been like hell for my mother.

All the boys went back to school, but it wasn't easy. Japan didn't have enough paper to print textbooks, so we received paper one sheet at a time, some of which was made of straw. The quality was so poor that when we tried to use an eraser on it we'd put a hole through it.

The small taste of American culture that the U.S. Navy men brought to Yokosuka really impressed me. I was especially awestruck by the printing quality on the wrappers of candies, cigarettes, chewing gum, etc. They had many vivid colors, even silver and gold. My eyes had been accustomed to only black and white printing for so long. I felt then that it was so silly to fight against a wealthy country

like the United States. Although I didn't realize it at the time, my hope to go to America was embedded in my heart.

It suddenly became very important to learn English, which I had neglected for so long. Every night I listened to the radio program by Tadaichi Hirakawa, which started with a song, "Come, come everybody..." I always associate this era of my life with this song and hunger.

Everyone wanted to learn English then. It was the thing to do. We gathered at a library run by CIE (Civil Information and Education) in Yokohama once a week, and listened to the story about America told by a famous comedian, Suisei Matsui. The American books and magazines inspired me every time I was there.

We formed a "Pen Pals Club" and exchanged letters with American teenagers. The American girls with blond hair that excited me back then when I looked at their pictures must be more than 50 years old now.

I had this outrageous plan: to try to understand broadcasts aimed at the occupation forces in Japan. I thought that this would be the best possible way to learn the American language. I set the dial to FEN (Far East Network) and listened to newscasts, comedies and other shows. The only words I understood were "hello," "goodbye," and "thank you." I also listened to baseball games, but all I could understand was "strike" and "out."

Disgusted, I had almost given up until I heard a very strange-sounding music. It was nasal-type singing, accompanied by a steel guitar, quite unlike Hawaiian music. Although the sound itself was very strange to my ears, I

liked it! I was able to understand the English words in the song because they were spoken much slower than the fast-talking radio show hosts. It was country music and the greats of the time were the late Hank Williams, Lefty Frizzel, Eddy Arnold, Tennessee Ernie Ford and Hank Snow. I listened to two programs daily, the "Twelve O'Clock Jamboree" and "Honshu Hayride." The first American song I learned was "You Are My Sunshine" and then the "Tennesse Waltz," but my love for country music increased with time and "Wedding Bells" and "Lovesick Blues" became my favorites.

We didn't have tape recorders back then so I jotted down the words to the songs one line at a time. It took several weeks for me to complete an entire song. My efforts paid off and I memorized more than 1,500 songs, while learning the English language at the same time.

The college entrance exams were drawing near and I wanted to major in hydromechanics to later apply to aerodynamics. I passed the written test for entrance to a very well-known university and was interviewed by several professors for admission. One of them was curious why I had planned to major in such an unpopular subject.

"I want to become an aircraft designer in the future," I said.

"Do you like airplanes?"

"Yes, I do. It was always my dream to become a fighter pilot, but we were defeated so it became impossible. My three brothers were all pilots, two of them lost their lives as Kamikaze pilots."

'So, this time you want to design the airplanes so they won't fall down," the professor replied with a cynical smile on his face.

His reply angered me. I shouted at him for making light of such courageous acts and, as you might have already guessed, I did not pass the exam. I sometimes wonder what I would be doing today if I had been a "good boy" and went into that field.

I attended some art and design schools after this incident, but was not totally fulfilled there either. There was still a part of me that felt empty and I began to fill my spare time listening to country music. Between classes at school, I started to sing professionally. I became well known in the area and was nicknamed the "Japanese Hank Williams" since I loved to sing his songs the most.

I was soon cutting records and appearing on stage and on TV shows, but the most pleasurable appearances I made were entertaining American forces at their camps all over Japan. The young, homesick boys from Southern states really enjoyed listening to their favorite music.

Backstage, after performing at the camps, I would look through *Playboy* magazines, which weren't sold to the Japanese public. I was, of course, enchanted by the beautiful women, but above all, I was impressed by the typography, illustrations, and overall graphic design of this magazine. I thought about how great it would be to work for such a magazine.

One rainy day in Tokyo, I was performing at a tea room with live music called "Paradise," when my eyes locked with those of a very beautiful girl. This was the start of my relationship with Yoshiko, my wife of 27 years.

After our first daughter, Risa, was born I evaluated what I was doing with my life. My singing career, when looked at realistically, was the same as an American boy singing Japanese songs for American customers in America. I am not saying this is good or bad, but there are definite limitations, so I decided to quit.

My wife and I opened a restaurant called the "El Paso" in a fashionable Roppongi area in Tokyo. Our specialty was American Southwestern dishes. We became acquainted with the Millers who had a dude ranch in Tucson, Arizona. We also saw Shibata again (he was my father's interpreter at Navy headquarters), who often visited for his favorite spareribs and also wrote a very nice critique of our restaurant in his newspaper.

I did not venture into the restaurant business without training. A year before opening, I had experienced all facets of the business from dishwashing to waiting tables and cooking at the Foreign Correspondents Club in Tokyo. I had been introduced to the Club through Koichi Obata, who had influenced me to love American culture.

The idea was good, but was also ahead of its time. I often make this kind of mistake. Many of the things I have done in my life were too radical or too soon. I also get bored easily doing the same thing for a long period of time. I am still unsure if this is a good or a bad quality.

The construction of subway systems in Tokyo for the 1964 Olympics had started and they closed many of the streets at night. Our restaurant business was dependent upon nighttime customers. I had been working as a designer during the day for "Staff, Inc.," an agency run by Obata, and also still sang occasionally on stage. All of these factors combined told me that I needed a change and I thought that it was the perfect time to cut off all ties and start anew.

I had always wanted to come to the U.S., especially since the end of the war, and it was time for me to test my talents as a graphic designer. So I packed my belongings, bought a one-way ticket, and with $500 in my pocket I boarded the President Cleveland in Yokohama in 1964. I still remember Yoshiko running beside the ship on that snowy March day. It was like a scene from a romantic movie—her running was kind of funny though.

LIFE IN THE U.S. (1964–)

It was a sunny day in April 1964. The cherry trees were in full bloom in San Francisco's Golden Gate Park, when I got off the ship and stepped onto American soil for the first time.

I had purchased a "See America" ticket, which enabled me to take any Greyhound bus for a year. I stayed in San Francisco and Los Angeles for a few days before going to Tucson, Arizona with Nobuyoshi Mori, who I met on the ship. He was on his way to Mexico. I looked up Grace and Howard Miller, who greeted us with open arms. I stayed with them for two weeks enjoying the Old West which I had only experienced through movies in the past.

There were many guests at the dude ranch. I was introduced by the Millers as the "Japanese Pat Boone." Children would follow me as I sang old American folk and cowboy songs for them. I also taught them a little Karate during my stay.

When I left, many of the guests invited me to stay with them if I was ever in the area where they came from. I took up these invitations and stayed with the Hollises in a suburb of Chicago and the Canfields in Madison, Wisconsin. John Canfield is the one who introduced me to someone working at Medalist Publishing Company in Chicago.

I interviewed with Tony Pronoitis, the art director, who had spent some time in Yokosuka when he was a young sailor. Of course I had never met him when he was in Japan, but perhaps his favorable impression of Japan made him decide to give me a chance as a designer with his company.

I came to the U.S. as a tourist, because that was the only way for me. If I got a job, my visa had to be converted to a working visa, which was next to impossible. Medalist sponsored me and requested my work permit from the immigration authority but the quota system from Japan was still enforced and I was almost deported after working in the U.S. for a year.

I didn't know where to turn. Yoshiko and Risa had joined me by now and we were living in an apartment close to Lincoln Park Zoo in Chicago. I was told that Canada was a possibility for finding work. I had almost made up my mind to go to Canada when I noticed that a branch of the Bank of Tokyo opened on LaSalle Street. I went inside and while browsing through a brochure I saw the name, Thomas Masuda. Masuda was a very well-established lawyer who Shibata of the Mainichi had told me to look up. They had been classmates in Washington.

I wrote a letter to Masuda explaining my situation and he assigned someone to handle my immigration matters. Immigration law at the time was very unfair to people from the Orient. If you were from Europe, especially England and Germany, you could come to the U.S. freely, but only 175 were allowed to come from Japan annually. With one exception: If you had a special talent that no unemployed American citizen could fulfill, you had a pretty good chance because you wouldn't be taking anyone's job away.

Masuda introduced me to a sales promotion and catalog studio, "Nobart," which was owned and operated by Noby Yamakoshi. The business dealt with some Japanese clients and we decided to convince the immigration office that they had a need for a designer that could speak, write, and read Japanese fluently. Well, not many Americans could fulfill that requirement. Nearly a year passed before I obtained an immigrant visa, commonly known as a green card. For this, I am forever indebted to a number of people who came to my aid in my time of need.

After receiving my card, I went into my boss's office to thank him for his support, but without a conscious effort, unexpected words came from my mouth. I said, "I would like to do more creative design, so I would like to resign."

Although I surprised Noby, I do believe that I shocked myself more. I had a wife and a small child and had not even looked for another job

8

yet. Perhaps some of you can appreciate and understand how I was feeling. If you have ever done catalog work I think you know. There is a lot of text, copy and photos without a lot of room for creative ideas and imagery. I felt as if I was locked in a very small room with no place to stretch.

With no job and three mouths to feed I called up Dick Helland who started his job at Medalist the same day I did but was now working for Cahners Publishing Company. He spoke with the art director and soon I was hired as art director for three construction-oriented magazines.

This is where I learned how to do table-top and architectural photography. It was a very good experience.

My second daughter, Chika, named after Chicago, the town where she was born, was one and a half years old when I got a sudden urge to buy a new car. We were living in the city and didn't really need one, but it was something that we could use with two children. I am an impulse spender. I made up my mind to settle for the very best, a Mercedes-Benz!

The winter of 1968 was cold and wet with heavy snow. Many of the schools and offices were closed for days at a time and after having already gone through a number of Chicago winters, the Golden State, California, attracted me. Again, Yoshiko, pregnant with our third child, had to follow her husband's fickle path,

accompanying me to yet another state. Looking back, I do believe that this was the scariest time in my experience.

We reached San Francisco Bay and stayed with friends there. I started freelancing at the agency where Rich Kaneko, our host, worked. I did many freelance jobs in the area and began to notice something. I saw that there were feelings that the Japanese people would work diligently for less money, and I got this feeling whenever I went on job interviews.

Although I was somewhat disappointed with my job situation, we enjoyed living there, making short trips almost every weekend south to Carmel, north to Bodega Bay, where Hitchcock filmed "The Birds," east to Lake Tahoe, and anywhere in between, stopping for wine-tasing and savoring delicious seafood. A friend in the East introduced us to the Aldens, who invited us to Mill Valley for a wonderful home-cooked dinner, and gave me leads to new accounts. I still remember the menu!

Dick Helland was in town from Chicago on business. We had dinner at the Playboy Club and he asked me if I wanted to go back to Chicago, because many people appreciated my work and missed me. Job satisfaction offset the climate conditions and I went back to Cahners again, after staying in San

Francisco for less than a year. Our third daughter was born before we left there. We named her Juri, meaning precious village, in dedication to that beautiful part of the country.

After coming back to Chicago, I did some job-hopping again, to CNA Insurance to Playboy Clubs International, and in 1975, I opened a small studio called Rising Sun. My future plans include publishing unique and unusual books as well as designing new and unique products.

I almost forgot to tell you why I changed my name to Yoshi. First, Yoshinobu is hard to pronounce and does not fit on a credit or business card. Secondly, Japanese characters for Yoshi mean "spared Samurai," and I was the only one of four brothers who did not experience becoming a fighter pilot.

Conflict Resolution

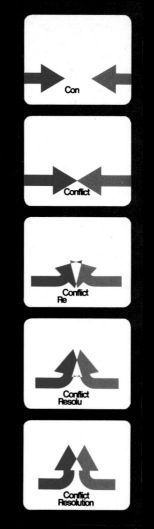

1

2

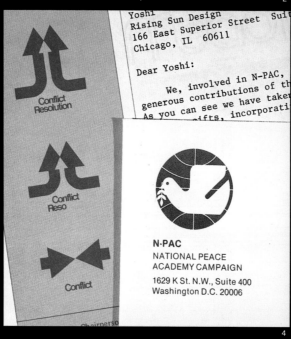

N-PAC
NATIONAL PEACE
ACADEMY CAMPAIGN

1629 K St. N.W., Suite 400
Washington D.C. 20006

4

3

5

U.S. PEACE INSTITUTE

If you were to judge me by the things I recall about the war, you might think I am militaristic. Nothing could be further from the truth. I am more qualified to be labeled a pacifist than most people. But at the same time, I feel that peace cannot be achieved by simply marching or praying for it. Peace among nations requires knowledge and understanding.

I can attest to that theory. I was born in Japan in 1931, and I remember things before, during, and after World War II. I was taught to hate foreigners, and was ready to die for the Emperor as a fighter pilot. Then I was exposed to country music, and came to the conclusion that people are basically the same all over the world. I have lived in and loved America for 23 years. Two of my daughters are natural-born American citizens.

Why did Japan go to war? Why did my two brothers and all the others have to fight and die? Wars are not fought between people. They are caused by misunderstandings, religious differences, and conflicts of interest in economics and history. Any government is capable of manipulating its people to hate foreigners.

The U.S. has Army, Navy, and Air Force academies to create key personnel. Yet it does not have an academy to promote peace.

These thoughts led a group of people to establish the National Peace Academy in 1976. Miyo Hayashi influenced me to do some design work for this movement. Hayashi was locked in a concentration camp during the war, even though she was an American citizen. She realizes how dangerous misunderstandings between two races can become.

The first thing that came to mind when I contemplated designing a symbol for the Peace Academy was a white dove with an olive branch. That is, after all, the universal symbol for peace. Then I realized it was too idealistic, just like some fake Buddhist monks dancing in the streets, or flower children who say beautiful things but evade responsibility to their country.

We decided to use the slogan "conflict resolution," and from that idea the final design was born. Two powers (represented by arrows) are about to crash, but avoid the collision by changing direction through mutual understanding. The third arrow, which appears in the middle, can be interpreted as peace, hope and happiness for all mankind.

1 *Final design based on slogan "Conflict Resolution."*
2 *Animated stages of two arrows emerging.*
3 *Early designs based on white dove and olive twig.*
4 *Examples of design applications.*
5 *This is the perception of peace for many people. Can we reach our goal this way?*

ntity Symbols in a recent issue of
vertising Age. I would be interested in
oking at your work and also getting some
pe of cost estimate on creating a new image
mbol for the Nebraska Air National Guard."

Japan, often designers are chosen only
cause they are personal acquaintances or
ends of friends. The opposite is true in the
S. where designers are usually selected on
e basis of their past record of achievement
d portfolio. Therefore, it is not unusual to be
ntacted by a total stranger.

he assignment appealed to me because
was for a highly visible governmental
ganization and because of my love for
rplanes and flying.

most creative and well-liked designs.

Although I was somewhat familiar with the
National Guard, there were many specific
facts to consider for the *Nebraska* Air
National Guard.

For example, I learned that the Air National
Guard is independent from the U.S. Air Force
and each state has one.

I also had to familiarize myself with the State
of Nebraska, which is in the center of U.S.
farmland and is famous for growing corn.

The Nebraska Air National Guard is
nicknamed Cornhusker Air Guard and the
word "cornhusker" is widely and proudly used

aircraft, used for reconnaissance activities,
is the F-4 Phantom.

After gathering all of the information that
I could find to meet my client's needs,
the next step was brainstorming for ideas.

My first design idea came to me as I looked
at the shape of the state itself. Nebraska is
shaped like a bald eagle which, of course,
is the symbol of the United States as well.
This I thought would satisfy my client's
request for an image that would be
recognized both statewide and nationally.

For the second design, I incorporated the
Nebraska state bird, the meadow lark, into

2

3

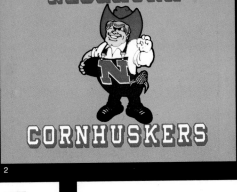

NEBRASKA AIR NATIONAL GUARD
HEADQUARTERS 155TH TACTICAL RECONNAISSANCE GROUP
LINCOLN MAP (ANG), LINCOLN, NEBRASKA 68524

REPLY TO
ATTN OF: RS/CRS

28 Jan 83

SUBJECT: State Identity Symbol

TO: Design 1
Div. of Rising Sun Design
437 Marshman Street
Highland Park, Ill. 60035

Dear Sir;

I am presently the advertising and public service director for the
Nebraska Air National Guard in Lincoln, Nebraska. In the recent
issue of Advertising Age I reviewed your ad concerning the corporate
identity symbol.

The Nebraska Air National Guard and the Air National Guard as a
whole, have been using the same logo for the past 10 to 15 years
(flag logo). We (Nebraska) have recently been using the "Hustlin'
Husker" logo as our unit or state identity. Neither of them create
an image to distinguish our military unit from others (I.E. Air
Force).

I would be interested in looking at your work and also getting some
type of cost estimate as to creating a image symbol that would be
identifing to our public service image, state image, and national
image.

Should you have any questions, please feel free to call me collect
at (402) 475-4910.

Sincerely,

Larry S. Brooks

LARRY S. BROOKS, MSGT, NEANG
Chief, Recruiting Services

READINESS .... IS OUR PROFESSION

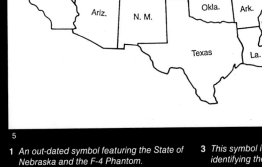

LARRY S. BROOKS
Lincoln Municipal Airport
Lincoln, Nebraska 68524
Business
LINCOLN (402) 475-4910
Autovon 948-1218
OMAHA (402) 294-5716
Home (402) 470-2813

THE NEBRASKA AIR GUARD

5

1 An out-dated symbol featuring the State of
Nebraska and the F-4 Phantom.

2 The Nebraska State College football team
logo depicts a "cornhusker." Note partially
husked corn in his pocket.

3 This symbol is recognized across the U.S.
identifying the National Guard.

4 The initial contact for a new corporate
identity symbol was made through the
mail in response to an advertisement in
Advertising Age.

5 Something as simple as the shape of a

incorporated a silhouette of an F-4 Phantom.

As anyone in the design business knows, their favorite or most inspirational idea is not always the most well-liked or final choice of the client. My favorite among the three design concepts for this project was the first one, the bald eagle, since it clearly defines the location and the nature of the organization immediately. Also, in my experience, the first idea that comes to mind is usually the best. The concept the client chose, however, was the last one — the corn and the F-4.

It can prove to be very interesting when you ask a client to explain the reasoning used in making a final decision. In this particular

the Iowa Hawks, caused its elimination from the choices.

After the design has been approved by the

to some great creative possibilities. All it takes is some knowledge of typography and good graphic sense.

Inspirations do not choose time or location. Sometimes a good idea pops up in the middle of the night and I end up conceptualizing and developing it into the wee hours of the morning. Often when inspiration strikes, there is nothing to write on or with. Many of my ideas are written on napkins, menus or anything else that I can get my hands on at the moment. My ideas for this design, for example, were drawn up on an airline ticket on my way home from Hong Kong.

Perhaps it was the sound of the jet engines or the environment itself that inspired me.

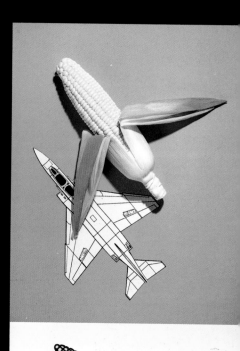

1

2

3

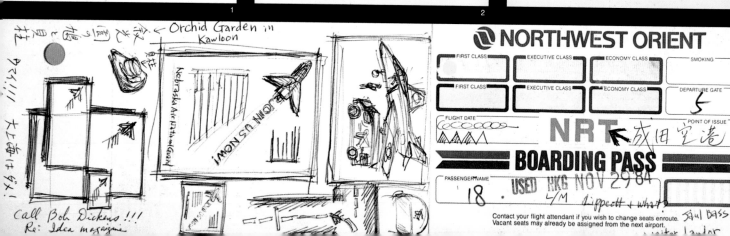

Call: 402/475-4910
NEBRASKA AIR GUARD

5   6   7

RECRUITING

8   9   10

1 The similarities between the bald eagle and the shape of Nebraska are brought together in the first design concept.

2 Just a few minor changes, initiating the state bird characteristics, resulted in the second design proposal.

3 Through photography, the third and approved concept was more easily visualized.

4 Ideas won't wait for the studio as this airline ticket proves.

5 The development of a decal makes this application to the F-4 possible.

6 The decal concept is applicable to just about anything—including helmets.

7 A recruiting poster adds a little extra dimension to the symbol with the "Join Now!" treatment that reveals the versatility of the design.

8 The letterhead, envelope and business card show what typography know-how can do for visual impact.

9 The identity symbol can be used for many things including directional signage in office areas.

10 Creative possibilities are unlimited. This promotional piece can actually fly and be sent flat inside an envelope.

11 The size and placement of the symbol will vary for different applications as shown here on the Phantom and van.

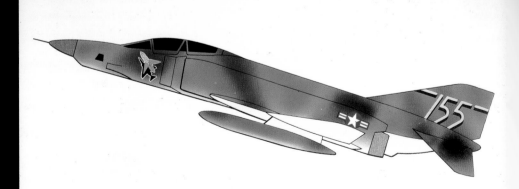

DAI-ICHI KANGYO BANK

Until 1976, Illinois banking law prohibited out-of-state banks from opening branches within the state. So when the Dai-Ichi Kangyo Bank (DKB) opened its doors in Chicago, it was named First Pacific Bank of Chicago. Henricus J.J. Vroegh, who heads the business development and advertising/PR departments at the bank, is a Dutch citizen.

When the bank started, trade between the U.S. and Oriental countries was not as commonplace as it is now, so its main emphasis was promoting services to businesses with import and export activities with Pacific countries. The ads and brochures designed reflected that policy.

Some people may say that I am a jack-of-all-trades, as I enjoy following through on a project from the initial concept to the finishing touches. This process includes conceptualization, design, layout, presentation, photography, and illustration—up to producing camera-ready art. If I assign someone else to do some of this work, I cannot be assured that I will be satisfied with the finished product.

The brochure shown below, for example, started out with a paper map that my daughter Risa (then in junior high) made objects on. I then depicted various countries using a Japanese-style Sumie (brush painting). In my opinion, these paintings should have been much looser. However, I was more conservative to suit my clients' taste. All

of the photographs, except for the one of Tokyo headquarters, were also taken by me, using bank employees as models. The exterior building shot was taken from the First National Bank of Chicago building. Using the competition's facility to promote First Pacific was quite ironic.

DKB became the largest bank in the world. The time had come for them to get back to their original and official name. I incorporated the "Superman" theme showing a conservative business suit and Superbank logo inside to create a powerful image. This concept was denied as the client thought it was too bold and immodest. So the final design was built around a map focusing on the bank's branches all over the world.

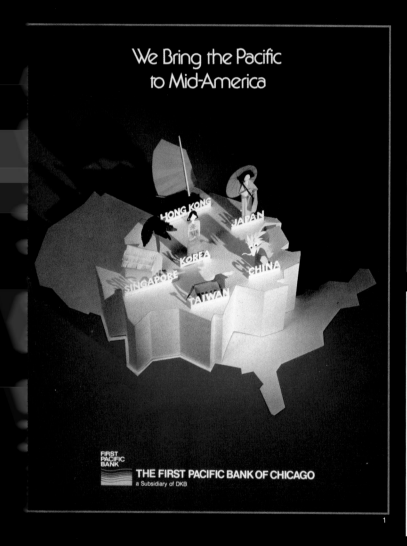

We Bring the Pacific to Mid-America

THE FIRST PACIFIC BANK OF CHICAGO
a Subsidiary of DKB

1

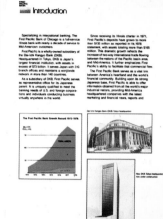

Introduction

2

3

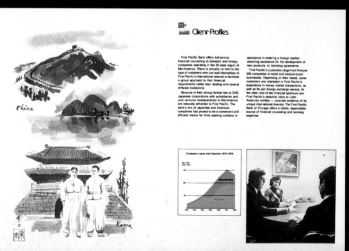

Client Profiles

Full Banking Services

1 *Capability brochure using the theme "We bring the Pacific to Mid-America."*

2-5 *Inside pages of the brochure showing Sumie paintings of each country.*

6 *With the simple idea of a jigsaw puzzle, the "First Pacific Bank solves the puzzle of Far East Business" theme was born.*

7 *An advertisement announcing DKB after its name change.*

8-10 *A brochure to accompany the ad, using different sized inserts to explain services.*

11 *The rejected "Superman" concept using a business suit and the bank's old logo.*

12 *An inside look at the "Superbank" brochure.*

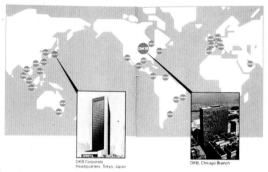

BANQUE NATIONALE DE PARIS

The Chicago branch of France's largest bank is architecturally pleasing, with brushed steel and smoked dark glass forming a very contemporary, sophisticated design . . . chic!

As you get off the elevator and walk toward the reception area, your eyes focus on the white, vertical, plastic panels with silkscreened characters spelling out Banque Nationale de Paris. An 18th Century Aubusson Chinese landscape tapestry greets visitors as they approach the end of the entrance corridor.

The tapestry serves to balance the rich tradition of the French with one of the most modern and efficient banks in the world.

In an effort to recreate this feeling in the brochure, I used different width pages to depict the plastic panels.

I took all of the photographs myself, with the exception of the shot of Paris Headquarters.

An exchangeable insert inside the back cover lists all current bank employees. It gives the piece a personal touch while extending the usefulness of the brochure.

1 *The bank logo was printed on silver stock giving it a rich and unique quality.*

2 *Four different width pages were bound-in to echo the scene of the entry area.*

3-5 *Inside pages focus on the bank's services and capabilities.*

6 *The inside back cover features an insert that can be updated as often as necessary, eliminating the expense of reprinting the brochure for minor changes.*

BNP   Banque Nationale de Paris

1

Welcome to BNP

2

BNP Paris/Chicago

BNP Services

3

BNP Markets

4

BNP Worldwide

5

BNP Tradition

BNP Management

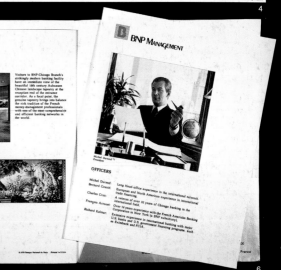

6

Build Yourself A Legend/Mark 3
MERCEDES-BENZ

By Don Swavely/ Yoshi Sekiguchi / Karl Ludvigsen

1

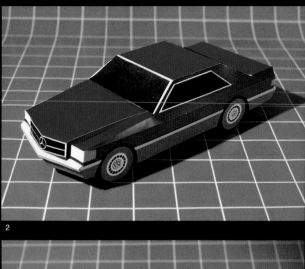

2

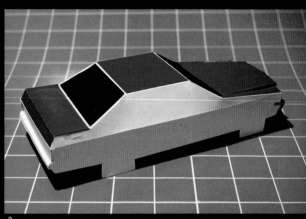

3

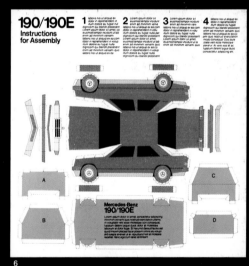

4

5

6

PAPER CAR PROJECT

Throughout my childhood, the magazines I loved to read were those with supplements between the pages. They had cut-out patterns to construct models, mainly of military planes. The fact that I could form a three-dimensional object out of a flat piece of paper fascinated me.

Perhaps because of the added printing expense, I had never seen this type of supplement used in the U.S. The U.S. is, however, big on putting premium items into boxes of candy and cereal without charge. I researched the history of paper models and their use as premiums in this country and found that General Mills had inserted a series of World War II fighter plane paper models in cereal boxes during the war. If you bought a box of Wheaties, you would find cardboard sheets inside with patterns of the Japanese Zero, P-51 Mustang, Spitfire and

Messerschmidt to cut out, glue and fly. Children loved making them and participating in national flying contests. Today you find plastic toys in the shape of cars, robots and monsters that don't require any assembly at all. Since when have children forgotten the joy of constructing a toy with their own hands?

I love cars, both real ones and models. I thought about whether or not people would buy books about cars if they contained patterns for paper-constructed models. There are many books like this on the market today which enable you to construct space shuttles, the Statue of Liberty and the Empire State Building while reading about them. However, most of them are complicated and require more than one piece of paper and a lot of patience.

By nature, paper can only bend in one direction and does not have the ability to form complex curves, such as a sphere,

1   *The cover made for the presentation shows the model cars rendered in felt tip pen, the actual finished piece would include photographs of the constructed cars.*

2   *The 560SE Coupe model photographed.*

3   *To save time in presenting the model concept, only half of the Mercedes-Benz model was completed.*

4   *The history of Daimler-Benz was to be included in the finished product.*

5   *C-111, made as a test bed for fast motoring.*

6   *The die-cut patterns shown on this page are inaccurate to prevent infringement.*

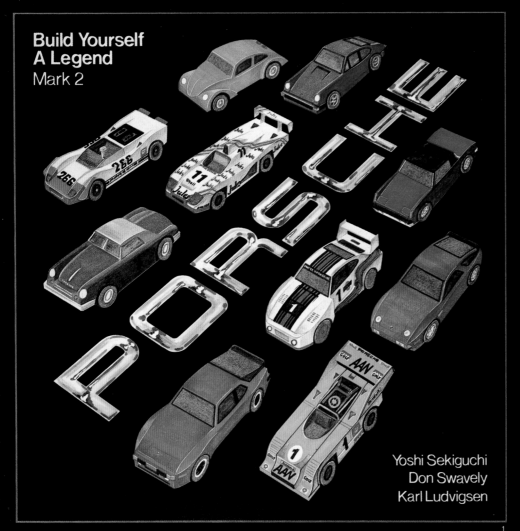

Build Yourself A Legend
Mark 2

Yoshi Sekiguchi
Don Swavely
Karl Ludvigsen

1

2

3

1 Ten representative models with logo for the Porsche version.

2-3 Note the sportier, lighter layout for the Porsche concept compared to the Mercedes-Benz.

4 Patterns for construction of the 944. The curves on the side make it more difficult to construct.

5 Here is proof that a caricature and a realistic drawing can be very similar.

6 Sportscars of the World version. Pictured here are 10 cars from 10 different manufacturers. The Nissan 280Z was chosen from Japan.

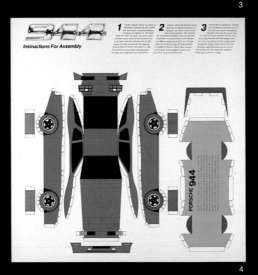

4

without the use of deep embossing. But compare a realistic portrait to a caricature of a person and you'll find that the caricature's simple lines often make a person easier to recognize than a realistic portrait.

This same principle applies to the art of impersonation. For example, my favorite country singer, Merle Haggard, once recorded a live performance in Philadelphia. On stage, he impersonated the greats like Marty Robbins, Hank Snow and Buck Owens. He amplified each singer's features and sounded more like them than they did, as strange as it sounds. Therefore, I thought, why can't stylized and exaggerated paper capture the essence of design, even if it doesn't look exactly like the real thing?

An example of styling or extracting essence can be seen in Oriental brush paintings. A simple horizontal line across the paper represents either the sky and the sea, or the sky and the plain. It all depends upon how one looks at it and on the individual's imagination. This Zen philosophy can also be applied to paper models.

I had to think of ways to market my new idea. My plan was to concentrate on one car manufacturer and publish a book with a brief history, photos and text of 10 representative models along with punch-out patterns to construct those cars. The book could be sold through bookstores as well as car dealerships.

The year 1986 marked the 100th Anniversary of Daimler-Benz, a perfect opportunity for me to test my concept. I created a very tight, comprehensive presentation to explain how the book would work. I collected books and researched the history of Daimler-Benz and chose my 10 representative models. The cover would picture the 10 constructed models along with the three-pointed star, a trademark of the German automobile manufacturer. Inside, several pages would tell the story of the manufacturer with two pages of photos and text on each model followed by a page of die-cut patterns for models measuring 6½ inches long in finished size.

The estimated printing cost was figured at $4 per copy for a 50,000 press run, the resale price was figured at five times that, or $20 per copy. It was a competitive price when compared to the $25 retail cost of posters today.

5

I constructed a model of the 560SE Coupe as a sample. In an effort to save some time, I constructed only half of a model, photographing it from different angles. The wheels were just the thickness of paper, without any depth.

Before I tried to locate a publisher for the book, I thought it would be helpful to secure some pre-publication sales from the manufacturer. The person in charge of Mercedes-Benz of North America was a friend of one of my old co-workers from the *Playboy* days. I sent the presentation along with the book proposal to his attention.

I planned ahead. Because it was possible that the proposal would be accepted I made an agreement with Don Swavely, an automobile model maker, to help me with this project. I wouldn't have time to do all of the work. Later, I received a reply from the PR director at Mercedes-Benz stating that their plans for the anniversary year were all locked into place and that there was no room for a new proposal.

I realized at this point that I had made my first mistake when I neglected to contact the right person in the company, the one who had the most power in the area of decision-making. The "don't make waves" saying could have been the culprit, meaning not to take unnecessary risks. If the project had been accepted and went well, the PR director would have gotten some credit for a job well done, but if it didn't go well, he might have lost his job. Well, I thought, if it doesn't work for Mercedes-Benz, I'll try Porsche. Both companies are based in the same city in West Germany, but avoid direct competition by making different types of cars. Perhaps Porsche lovers would be a more suitable audience to this type of book.

This time I constructed a 944 model Porsche with a finished underbelly and thick tires, which stood inspection well from all angles. The design theme was much lighter and sportier than the Mercedes-Benz, reflecting a different style. I was determined not to make the same mistake again!

Since many books had already been written about Porsche, I thought that if I contacted the authors of some of these books and worked with them it might go more smoothly since these authors already had publishing connections. I chose four authors, two in the U.S., one in England and one in Germany and I wrote them, without including graphic materials in order to shield my concept.

Karl Ludvigsen, an author who's *Porsches: Excellence was expected* is considered the bible for Porsche enthusiasts, offered his support to write the text for my book. However, the publishers that have put out many of his books did not share his enthusiasm and were not interested in publishing the book. My plan had again failed!

There is a saying that the poorest shot will eventually hit the target if he shoots often enough. Therefore, I decided to widen my area of prospective buyers.

Other than the two books that I had already assembled, I also worked on calendars with 12 cars. The concept is that you can construct a model car after the month is over. In Japan, calendars are mainly used as promotional media and they are often offered free of charge, but in this country, nicely printed calendars can cost $20 to $30.

This time I wrote to editors of three major automotive magazines, *Car & Driver*, *Road & Track* and *Motor Trend*. Each of these publications has a circulation of about 750,000 and they also print calendars and posters. John Dinkel, the editor of *Road & Track*, liked my idea so much that he introduced me to a publishing section of CBS. They thought the idea was excellent, but after serious consideration came to the conclusion that the break-even point would be 20,000 copies, which the sales force could not guarantee.

19

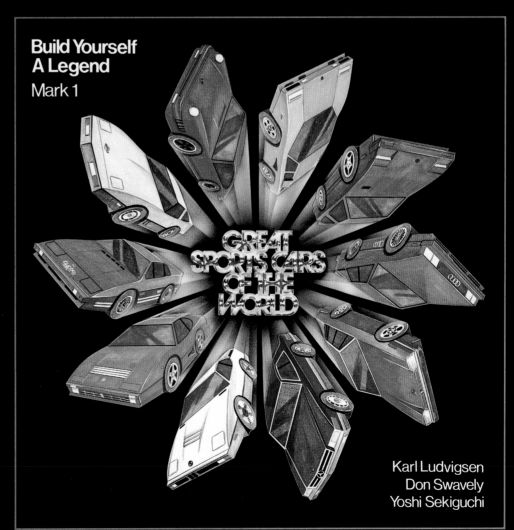

Build Yourself A Legend
Mark 1

GREAT SPORTS CARS OF THE WORLD

Karl Ludvigsen
Don Swavely
Yoshi Sekiguchi

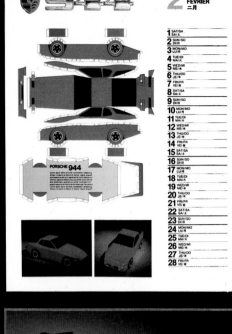

1

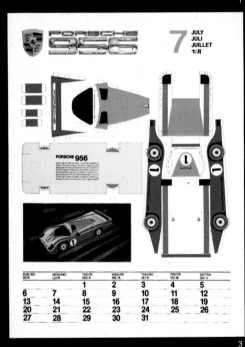

3

4

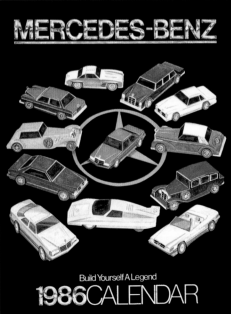

5

6

I did not stop there, I also sent out letters and proposals to manufacturers of automotive parts such as tires, car radios, batteries, and replacement parts suggesting that they use my idea to advertise their products. I received three polite rejections out of 60 proposals.

This, I thought, was the last straw and I was ready to give up the whole thing when I heard that David E. Davis, former editor of *Car & Driver*, was starting a new car buff magazine, *Automobile*. He had the financial support of Rupert Murdock, who had been buying newspapers, publishing houses and TV stations across the U.S. I wrote him a letter asking if the new magazine could use my project for promotion and this time I took a chance and included slides of page layouts and model cars.

Three weeks had passed when I got a call from New York. Mel Berger, the advertising director of the magazine, told me that they liked my idea and wanted to use it for promoting to advertisers. They wanted to start with a series of four cars, beginning with the Corvette.

My body was weightless with joy and I ran around in circles shouting for several minutes. It was not because my project would make money, but because someone saw the value of my concept and appreciated it after three long years of hard work.

It was just before the holiday season of 1985 when I went to New York to confirm my project plans with Mel Berger. Our 26th wedding anniversary was coming up, so Yoshiko joined me and we took a suite at the Waldorf Astoria, where our Emperor had stayed. It was a very happy occasion.

I brought actual sized designs of books and calendars along with two completed models for a presentation. Mel fell in love with them. He told me he had shown some of the slides to people from Porsche that morning, and they flipped!

We discussed expenses, time and cost. I did not want to give up the copyright to my patterns, so the magazine had a one-time publication right. I took this precaution so that I would be able to use my patterns in the future for books and calendars. Now the actual work began.

7

8

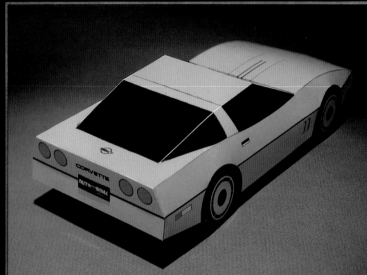

9

Every little detail counted now. I was asked to design the patterns so that people could assemble them without glue or paste. I wasn't quite sure how I was going to physically do this, since the simplest of shapes, such as a box, requires some glue.

For about three months I tried out a countless number of patterns. Without the use of glue, each piece of the pattern had to fit precisely with tabs and slits. Going around the area of the wheels was the most difficult part and it took a lot of trial and error, over and over again.

Again, I was ready to give up hope that I would ever get it right. I almost returned the advance payment and scratched the project. But one morning, while still half asleep, a solution occurred to me. I went straight to work and tried it . . . it worked!

I made up a prototype slightly larger than actual size, colored it, photographed it from various angles and sent it out. It was a good feeling, yet also sad. This project had become my baby.

Mel called and said it was gorgeous. Some manufacturers also voiced interest in using the model to introduce new cars. After all, the average ad in a magazine gets 15 seconds of reader exposure. By constructing a model and displaying it, it could be weeks or even months before its effectiveness wears off.

Who knows, perhaps one day my original concept of a car book with paper models may come to fruition.

10

1 Porsche calendar cover. Two cars were added, one a just-released 959 model.

2 944 for February. English, German, French and Japanese were used for the months and days of the week for international adaptation.

3 956 for July. The most widely used model for races.

4 The 944 and 956 paper models.

5 The Mercedes-Benz calendar cover.

6 Sportscars of the World calendar cover.

7 Many patterns were tried before the final Corvette model was complete.

8 This prototype of the Corvette was colored with Pantone overlays.

9 Rear view reveals Automobile magazine's logo.

10 The newly published Automobile magazine.

STANDARD RATE & DATA SERVICE

Media buyers in advertising, publishing, public relations and direct marketing rely on the 14 books published by SRDS, a Macmillan company, based in Wilmette, Illinois.

These publications are, by far, the most valuable source of information for the pros as well as the everyday person seeking to market a new product or start a new business.

For example, if I invented a revolutionary fishing lure, how many prospective buyers could I reach with a budget of $100,000? You might think that this kind of information is almost impossible to obtain without knowing where to start. But, by using Standard Rate & Data Service, a magic door to the world of marketing opens up as easily as a magician would say ''Open, Sesame'' and gets results.

Let's look into the consumer publication edition. Open to the section on ''Fishing and Hunting'' and all major magazines, such as ''Field & Stream,'' and other related magazines are listed with information on advertising rates, closing dates, circulation data, editorial content and even personnel. Magazines not directly related to fishing, but to other industries such as boating and tourism, are also listed as cross references in this section. These lists are updated monthly. If I divided the ad rate by the circulation I would get the CPM or cost per thousand and I would be able to figure how much it would cost to reach one reader. If I were to check the

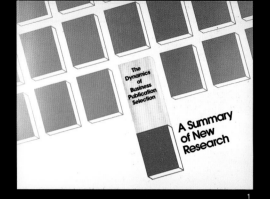

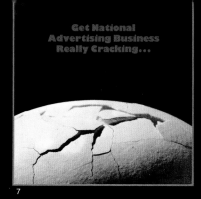

7

8

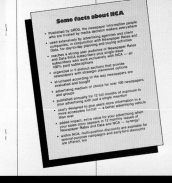

9

10

business publication edition, I would know how to reach the professionals in the fishing industry. I could also get data on advertising in area newspapers where the fishing activity is high, locally or seasonally. I can even get a list of people who have purchased fishing equipment in the past two years.

In other words, by using the resources provided by SRDS, I could market my lure in the United States from anywhere in the world.

The circulation of SRDS publications is at the saturation point. They have no competition. Many other firms tried to start up a similar service, but they all failed. It takes a lot of capital and manpower to maintain and update the vast amount of information contained in these publications.

You might think that it's silly for a company without any direct competition to conduct high quality promotional and advertising campaigns. That is where this company shines. I got involved in working for SRDS from one phone call. Nancy Hicks, who got my name from someone who I had worked with at Cahners Publishing, called and asked to see my portfolio. Later, she told me that she had actually been given three names, but called me first since my name sounded the most creative and interesting. I never knew that one's name could have such an influential power.

A team of very talented writers and production personnel under the supervision of Janis Wilson at SRDS, never fail to come up with very unique concepts. In order to make users understand their services completely, offbeat themes like rare animals, eggs and cartoons are chosen. I was responsible for making these concepts work visually.

Unfortunately, my original contact with SRDS recently moved to Atlanta. Perhaps someday I will get a phone call from Georgia with an exciting new project.

1-6 *Research data, "Magazines, the agency selection process," was designed with progressive dividers for each section expressing the feeling of process.*

7 *First of a series of ads. "Magazine travel advertising takes off . . . with SRDS."*

8-9 *A corresponding brochure was mailed out after the*

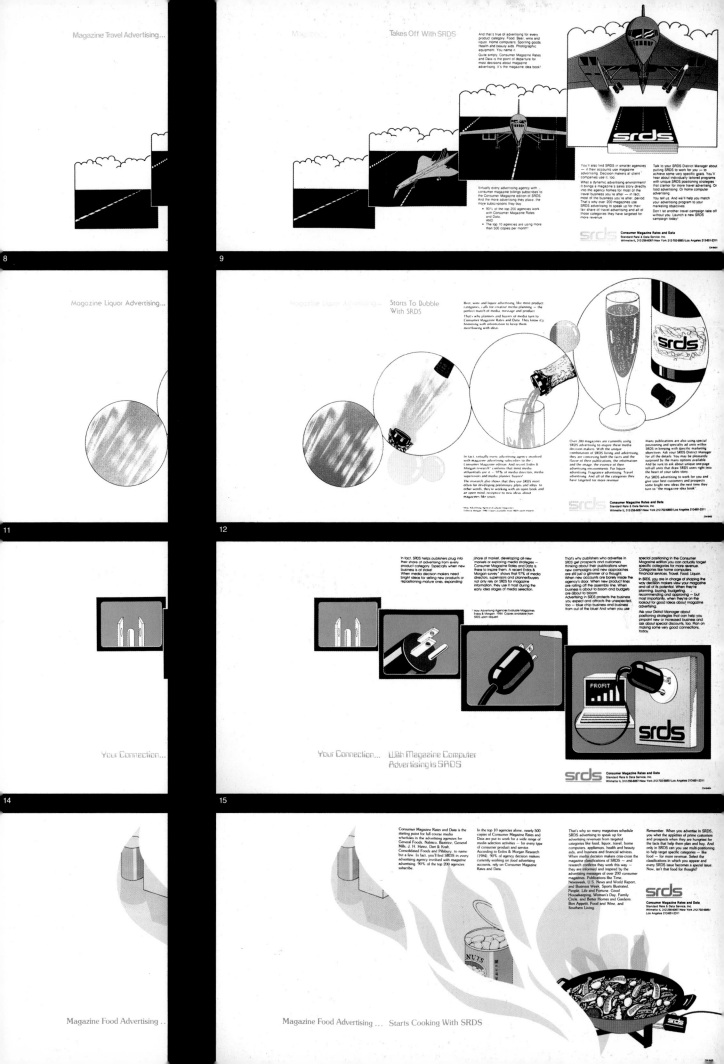

VIP MAGAZINE OF PLAYBOY

VIP, according to Playboy's dictionary, means Very Important Playboy. VIP magazine was published four times a year for club members, called keyholders. Its purpose was to report on new activities of the Playboy Empire.

I joined the magazine in the fall of 1971, and the first issue I worked on was the spring issue of the following year.

The big news item for this issue was the introduction of the newly opened hotel in Great Gorge, New Jersey. It was situated atop a very beautiful, hilly terrain with magnificent golf courses. We needed to get photographs for the cover and inside pages, so this was the first of many business trips for me while working for Playboy.

I worked four years at Playboy and during that period the ''Empire'' was at its peak. With his hotels and casinos, books, movies, records and 22 clubs, Hugh Hefner was flying all over in his private black jet with the rabbit symbol painted on the tail. I always wanted to work for Playboy so this was my dream come true.

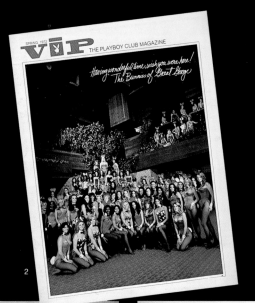

Hefner inspected every page of *VIP* magazine as well as *Playboy* magazine. It was just as important to him because it gave keyholders an inside look at the corporation. When I presented him with layouts they were almost as complete as the printed page. Actual photos were scaled and cropped into position, headlines were actually set, and suggested text was neatly typewritten and attached. It was a time-consuming task but when the layout was approved, all I had to do was set the type and paste it down. The actual production was handled by Bruce Hansen who is now an associate art director of *Playboy* magazine.

I always left a 3-inch margin around the page design for Hefner's changes or remarks. If I got it back without any marks at all it meant that it was approved, if he wrote "O.K.," then it was good. I was puzzled when one day my page layouts were returned with his signature and the comment "Good Spread." I wasn't aware of it at the time, but according to those who worked for Hefner for a long period of time, this remark is equivalent to an Oscar or Nobel Prize.

1

28

2

3

4

5

1-3 *The first televised "Bunny of the Year." Judges chose one of 22 contestants.*

4-6 *The next year, we concentrated on reporting more on the bunny's private life than on the show itself.*

7 *The first of the drink series. I used a small globe to interpret the world of vodka.*

8 *Using a wide-angle lens, these bottles of wine were shot straight down. The pages were designed using a background, camera angle and lighting not usually found in commercial photography.*

9-14 *Different drinks for different seasons.*

15 *Chan, Izui and myself worked together on this series. Those pictured are now models for the Japanese edition of* Playboy.

The World of Vodka

Vodka, according to the ads, will leave you breathless. This pitch has a particular appeal for executives who from time to time return to their offices after important wet business lunches and, in a sense, the pitch's true. Vodka *will* leave you breathless. It will also, if you drink too much of it, leave you speechless and motionless.

In this country, vodka was originally a drink for people who were looking for fireworks without flavor. But, while there are still people who enjoy the effects but dislike the taste of strong liquors, an ever-growing segment of the drinking population now loves vodka for vodka's sake.

By Federal definition, vodka must be so treated "as to be without distinctive character, aroma or taste." Why not, then, buy the cheapest vodka—on the assumption that they're all alike—and be done with it? Because distilling is a very complicated process that involves all kinds of sophisticated equipment, and two distillers, like two chefs, will seldom come up with identical products—even when they are following the same recipe. Further, little that passes over our taste buds is truly tasteless, and the *(continued on page 34)*

7

Invitation to a Wine Tasting

In those distant Biblical days it was sufficient to advise "a little wine for thy stomach's sake," and let it go at that. But in today's wine-conscious society, the knowledgeable host has to come up with something a bit more comprehensive and extensive.

The problem is, of course, that many Americans simply haven't had the opportunity to sample a great variety of wines and have had few chances to compare vintage against vintage or bottler against bottler.

There are, happily, a great many ways to expand experience while having a very good time, and one of the most pleasant and entertaining of these is to hold what the Germans call a *Weinprobe*, or wine-testing.

And good advice on how to go about it is readily available: Our resident wine expert, Philippe Massolo, Food and Beverage Director for Playboy Clubs and hotels, is a Frenchman who knows his wines—from his native Riviera to the Rhine-bordering province of Alsace, where he spent many childhood summers—and he enjoys talking about them. Here's his prescription for a wine-tasting party:

"You should draw up a list of eight to ten guests. That's about the number of glasses you get from the standard 75-centiliter bottle. And you'll need about 40 glasses. They need not be fine crystal, but they should be stemmed and round-bellied to permit the bouquet to develop.

"Then you should select the wines. And by this I don't mean a bottle of sherry, a bottle of California red, a chianti and *(continued on page 44)*

8

A Cheer for Beer

here's to a summer classic

9

BOURBON the all-american drink

10

Knockout Punches

for your big autumn bash, try this pair of cooling concoctions

11

Sunrise for Tequila

a change of pace, a change of taste

12

Beginning a Perfect Ending

liqueurs that invite you to linger awhile

13

Cocktail Classics

14

15

1-2 *Business conventions and parties were often held at the Playboy hotels. Here, Kikkoman soy sauce held a big party to celebrate its opening of a factory in Wisconsin.*

3 *I met many celebrities in my years at Playboy. Here, the late Mr. Ushiba, then ambassador from Japan, is pictured.*

4-5 *If there is no news, create it! A staged demonstration was planned with the bunnies fighting for the right to date customers.*

6-8 *A bunny holiday in Jamaica.*

9 *Not all bunnies are relaxed when photographed. I sometimes had to joke around with them to make them feel more comfortable.*

10 *''Bunnies of Miami.''*

11 *''Bunnies of the West.''*

12 *''Tonight in the Penthouse...,'' shows entertainers at Playboy clubs and hotels.*

30

The magazine content included the latest news, an entertainment calendar and a 10-page section called "The World of Playboy." Pictorial reports on events such as the "Bunny of the Year" could be planned ahead of time. News on new movie productions, conventions, and impressions on the clubs by cartoonist Arnold Ross were sometimes featured. Later, a drink feature was added, photographed by very talented inside photographers such as Pompeo Posar, Dwight Hooker, Don Azuma, Dick Izui and David Chan. I designed each scene and directed the shootings.

A very valuable lesson I learned through my work with Playboy was to go after the best result and not skimp expenses. They told me that film is the cheapest expense, so when in doubt, try different angles and bracket exposures. Testing took more time than actual shooting. A typical playmate session took several hours and sometimes the models themselves would yawn and even fall asleep.

Once I got used to the magazine schedule I had a hard time keeping myself busy, so I started to plan new features for the pages. Not just showing facilities of a hotel but bringing in bunnies and building stories around them. So we brought Carol, bunny of the year from the Miami Club, to the Jamaica Hotel. My family came along with me and we spent a week in a tropical paradise working and vacationing.

Other features we came up with included photographing bunnies in their own clothing, and focusing on their talents or hobbies.

I have a hard time today calling my years with Playboy work. It was a pleasurable and valuable experience. In my travels I was able to meet famous people in person and many other people who have helped me in my career.

VIP magazine ceased publication in 1975. It is kind of ironic that shortly after that, the Playboy empire went downhill. Recently, all remaining clubs were closed except for those that are franchised. They still live on in my fond memories.

Bunnies of MIAMI

meet six cottontails from our florida hutch

Holding Up A Diaper

Any mother should remember when a safety pin somehow managed to disappear under a sheet, a blanket or anything, at the very time when she was changing a diaper.

Thank Goodness, today's disposable diapers don't depend on safety pins. They are constructed and assembled with hot-melt adhesives and secured to babies with the help of adhesives tapes.

Here, ARKON, a tackifying resin from Arakawa is hard at work. Its outstanding properties of compatibility, heat-resistance, transparency and non-toxication make it ideal for use in pressure-sensitive tapes and labels, hot-melt bonding agents, sealants, mastics and latex systems, etc.

It's FDA approved, and no wonder why so many manufacturers of disposable diapers favor ARKON for their adhesives.

Happy mothers don't have to look for safety pins anymore, and harried adhesive formulators can find their answers in the line of products from Arakawa.

For further information, please write or call:

ARKON®

ARAKAWA Forest Chemical Industries, Ltd.

Chicago office:
5940 West Touhy Avenue
Niles, Illinois 60648
Phone: (312) 647-7797

It's SUPER Ester...

FIGHTING AGAINST OXIDATION: Super Ester A is processed by a special method giving it increased stability and excellent antioxidation qualities. Super Ester A is super-stable and resistant to aging so it maintains its color and quality during storage and application.

RESISTING HEAT: Super Ester A is heat-resistant allowing only minor heat loss. Used in hot melt and pressure sensitive adhesives, Super Ester A is odorless, less volatile, and doesn't change color.

FIGHTING FOR COMPATIBILITY: Super Ester A is highly compatible with SBR, acrylic polymers, chloroprene and thermoplastic rubbers, resins, and EVA resins.

Super Ester A by Arakawa is the natural tackifier . . . derived from pine trees . . . one of nature's renewable resources. So, unlike hydrocarbon resins, Super Ester A is readily available; there's no uncertainty of supply. And Super Ester A can be used in place of polyterpene resin and hydrogenated rosin ester.

FIGHTING OXIDATION, RESISTING HEAT, FIGHTING FOR COMPATIBILITY . . . it's *SUPER* Ester.

Arakawa Chemical Industries, Ltd.

Head office:	Chicago office:	Hamburg office:
1-21 Hirano-machi Higashi-ku, Osaka 541 Japan Phone: (06) 209-8500	625 North Michigan Avenue Chicago, IL 60611 U.S.A. Phone: (312) 642-1750	2 Hamburg 11, Kajen 2 F R Germany Phone: (040) 364275

ARAKAWA CHEMICAL

Maybe it's because I do not promote myself much, but I only have a few Japanese clients. I think it's partly because Japanese businessmen in the U.S. tend to prefer American agencies and designers over their Japanese counterparts. Sometimes Japanese companies pay dearly for advertising and fail to convey their message.

It is ironic because if an American company went to Japan, and found an American designer who had been working there for more than 20 years among the top Japanese designers, they wouldn't think twice about hiring him.

Mack Harashima knows this situation, and unlike many Japanese, he does not subconsciously feel inferior to the white race.

Mack is the head of Arakawa's U.S. headquarters. He attended Japan's Gakushuin and Florida State University. He is one of those rare people who has a college degree from two different countries.

Products from Arakawa Chemical are used by major companies in the U.S. and considered the best in their respective fields. They have received an excellent response to their advertising campaign here. I am glad that my design is indirectly helping Japan, and that many American people are enjoying life more by using Arakawa's products.

How to Win A Tackifier Game

Arakawa, the manufacturer of ARKON resins has the answer.

Our newly developed SUPER ESTER S-80, S-100 and S-115, three aces in a hole, are light in color, low volatile, very stable in high temperature and highly compatible with resins, thermoplastic rubbers, EVA resins and above all, acrylic polymers.

The SUPER ESTER series when used as a tackifier in hot melt adhesives, pressure sensitive adhesives (solvent-based or hot melt-based) will show an advantageous performance and is sure to make you a true winner!

For more information, please write or call our offices.

Arakawa Chemical Industries, Ltd.

Chicago Office: 625 North Michigan Avenue, Chicago, IL 60611
Phone: (312) 642-1750
Hamburg Office: 2 Hamburg 11, Kajen 2, F R Germany
Phone: (040) 364275

Circle No. 6 on Reader Service Card.

It Absorbs!

Introducing Arasorb. The super absorbent polymer.
Now anything that can't absorb up to 850 times its weight in liquid isn't as super.

Arasorb® super absorbent polymer is a revolutionary breakthrough for all your absorbency and containment applications.

And we've got the test scores to prove it. Test scores that show Arasorb® has a superior absorption rate and capacity in comparison to cellulose, starches and other organic materials. For example, Arasorb® absorbs over 850 times its weight in water.

And unlike other conventional materials, Arasorb® becomes a gel when wet. So liquids are contained without leakage. Even under pressure.

So now with Arasorb® you can give exceptional security against leakage. And exceptional slimness to your product. Without

giving up effectiveness. And that can mean exceptional comfort for your customers.

Which all can mean exceptional sales success for you.

And because Arasorb® is non-toxic, it gives a clear competitive advantage to the makers of sanitary napkins, disposable diapers and incontinence products. Plus Arasorb® is used for a whole range of other innovative consumer and industrial applications.

In fact, Arasorb® will absorb just about anything your imagination can pour into it.

So contact us now with your specific requirements.

Arakawa Chemical, USA

625 North Michigan Avenue, Chicago, IL 60611 Phone: (312) 642-1750

JAPAN	EUROPE	TAIWAN
1-21, Hiranomachi Higashi-Ku, Osaka 541 Japan Phone: (06) 209-8580	2 Hamburg 11 Kajen 2 F R Germany Phone: (040) 36-4275	Room No. 701, No. 152 Section 1 Chung Shan North Road Taipei, Taiwan Phone: (02) 531-7897

1 Ad for Arkon. The product is widely used for disposable diapers and sanitary napkins.

2 The Superman theme was used to promote Super Ester, a tackifier. I covered part of the "S" symbol to avoid possible trouble.

3 Four major products from the company represent a winning hand.

4 Ad for Arasorb, a super absorbent powder.

5 Logo now in use (left) and proposed logo.

1

2

CORPORATE IDENTITY PROGRAM FOR ROYAL HOST

Royal Host, a restaurant chain similar to Golden Bear or Denny's, decided to launch a corporate identity program. A noted designer in Japan and personal friend of mine for 15 years, Koichiro Inagaki, came to me with the assignment. I first met him when he visited Playboy with Kodansha's intention of publishing a Japanese edition.

Royal Host branched out from its parent, Royal Company, in the early 1970s. Kyoichi Egashira, the head of Royal Host, is quite an interesting individual. At the end of the war he returned home to find the fortune his father had accumulated was totally worthless. He had no alternative but to support himself by becoming a cook at the Itazuke U.S. Air Force Base. There he learned efficiency and management—American style. His experience as a cook led to where he is today.

In a way, his story resembles mine. My family also lost everything in the war, and I entertained American pilots at the same base. Our paths may have even crossed at one time back then.

By the time this project was started in the late 1970s, the company already had a logo. But that was when the company planned to start expanding, and needed a professional-looking symbol. They had even considered renaming the chain "Royal's", so we were instructed to prepare ideas for incorporating this possibilty also.

1 *Exterior shot used for annual report in English.*
2 *Transitional use of logo in all capital letters.*
3 *Old logo with exterior and interior scenes*

ROYAL HOST

営業時間　あさ8：00〜よる24：00

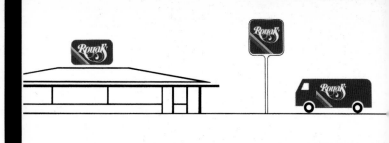

1

2

3

4

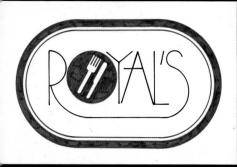

5

6

7

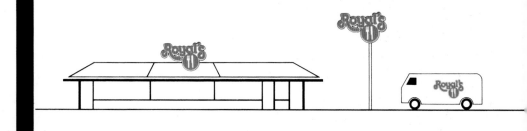

8

9

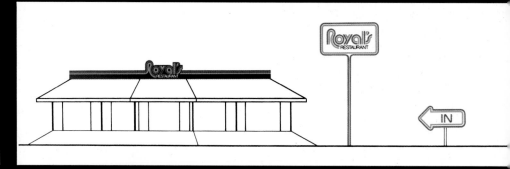

10

11

-4 Three proposals and an application. (Design by Jim Lienhart).

5-9 Four proposals and an application. (My designer friend's work).

0-13 One of my designs. Different color combinations were used to represent departments.

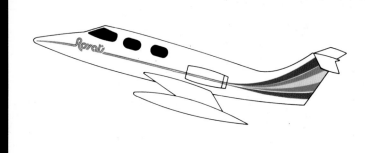
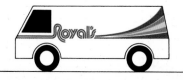

As an American expression, "Royal Host" connotes a very formal and aristocratic atmosphere. Japanese people have a somewhat different idea of its meaning. For the Japanese, "Royal Host" means nothing more than a restaurant that treats you with the utmost care. This created a hangup for the team of American designers that I worked with. They wanted a version incorporating an elegant typeface in royal blue with a hint of a sash with medals.

Jim Lienhart and a designer, who will remain nameless because he did work for a major competitor, submitted a few designs. I built around a square serif typeface, which I modified from an existing face. The style gives you a feeling that the company is dynamic and dependable.

In the end, the management decided against changing its name and in favor of the typeface I submitted. At the same time, they proposed creating a "cute" animal symbol to appeal to young childen. I assigned three talented cartoonists to the project. Later they decided against the plan. They thought a cartoon symbol might hurt Royal Host's high class image. The decision was right, I believe, because Japanese people have an attitude about serious elegance that is similar to the Europeans'.

If there is such a thing as color psychology, I subscribe to it. I selected a dramatic orange for the logotype since warm colors supposedly make your appetite grow. On the contrary, cool colors are supposed to calm you down.

After they had settled on one design, work on an application manual began. Even a good logo, or symbol, can be spoiled if used poorly. It takes both time and expense to complete the manual, but after you have one together, you don't have to think about how to apply the logo design. The manual should give guidelines for everything from a large outdoor sign to a match book cover.

It took three months to complete the manual. I even applied the logo to a Lear jet, with the foresight and hope that Egashira, an ex-pilot, would be in the position to fly around in it.

1

3

1 Sketches done by Chicago-area cartoonists. The plan to apply "cute animals" as a symbol was abolished.
2 Different colors for each function.
3 This typeface was the one chosen to be used with Royal Host's logo.

Peoples' perceptions and overall situation differ in Japan, so a certain thing that works for someone in the U.S., may not be applicable in Japan, and vice versa. In that case, the application can be modified, keeping the overall purpose and meaning the same.

Even after living in Western culture for 23 years, I still find it very difficult to understand at times. When we visited the Mercedes-Benz factory to pick up our car in 1968, we had lunch in their classy restaurant. Every single item on the table was adorned with the famous MB symbol, the three-pointed star. The company logo was even woven into the fabric of the bathroom towels. Being a curious person, I peeked in one of the stalls, and there

it was! The logo was printed on the toilet paper. Could you use toilet paper with your family crest, or company logo imprinted on it? It would make more sense to me if you used your competitor's logo.

I had a chance to visit Japan two years after I completed the manual and Mr. Inagaki took us to some of the Royal Host restaurants. The application examples were not perfected yet, but judging by the overall employee attitude, I was confident that they would follow through.

I have past restaurant experience and also worked for a leading magazine in the industry, so I understand how fierce the competition is. By eating in a restaurant just once, I can judge whether it will be a success or not. My judgement is mostly based on the overall

quality of food and service. Royal Host, I thought, would be the best and largest chain in Japan. Not only because of fine food and service, but also because it has the potential to export Japanese hospitality in true meaning, and the ability to succeed in establishing restaurant chains all over the world.

Several years passed and the Royal Host logo applications became standard. The orange cut-out logotype fits very nicely to either a typical family restaurant, a modern building in a downtown business area or an East Coast cottage-style building. I realize it is somewhat difficult to esthetically apply one logo to widely varying buildings, but in this case, they have succeeded.

1

2

3

4

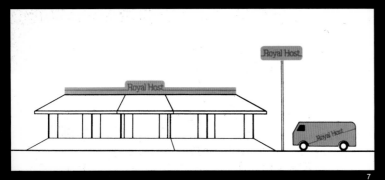
5

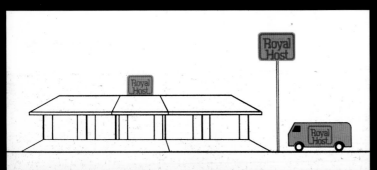
6

1-10 *Various combinations of the same typeface showing four different cases of its application.*

11-26 *Pages from the application manual. This takes time and effort, but once completed, the logo can be applied to almost anything automatically and consistently.*

7

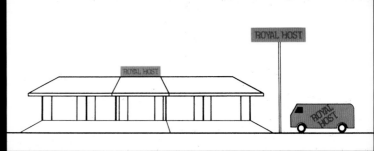
8

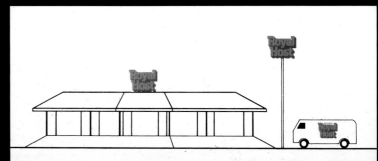

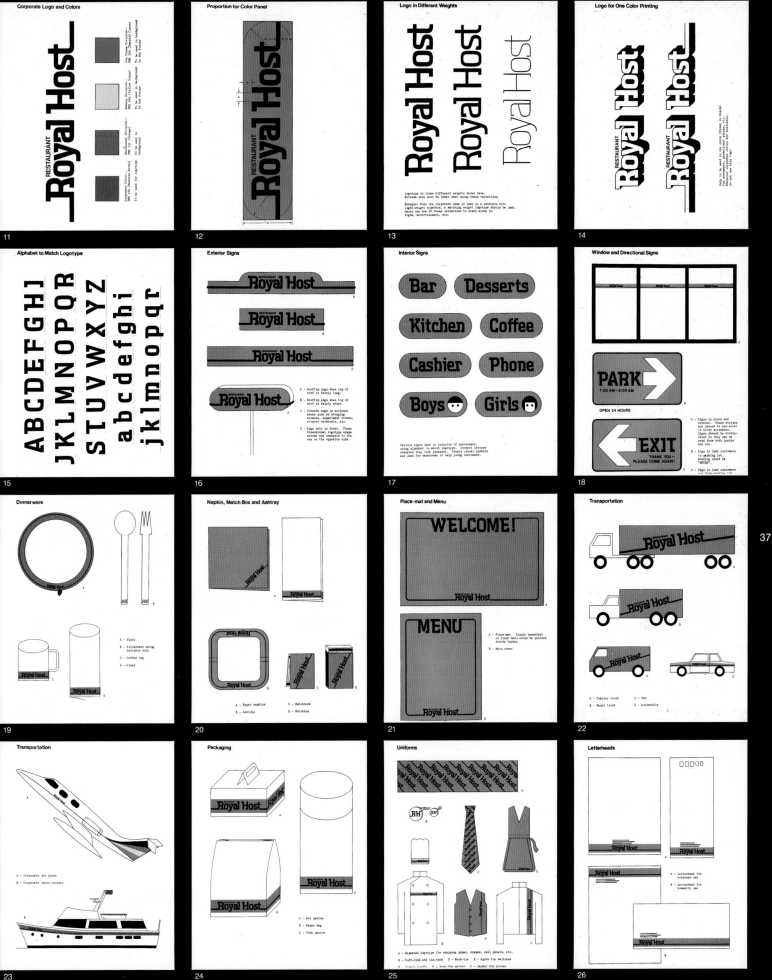

It is interesting to realize that Royal Host has never developed a logotype in Japanese, especially when the logo is displayed with McDonald's logo in Japanese. Maybe the reason for success lies here. Royal Host targeted families with higher education, stuck to the English logotype to keep a high image, imported American corporate identity technology, and made an effort to satisfy customers with fine food.

You can purchase stocks of this restaurant, which proves the company is very stable.

LOGO DESIGN FOR BECKER'S

I received an international phone call from Mr. Inagaki stating that Royal was starting a chain of fast food restaurants to compete with McDonald's. They were naming the chain Becker's, meaning baker in German. They were seeking a logo design for the chain and asked for my assistance after rejecting a presentation made by Dentsu. Imagine that, a guy like me competing with an all time great like Dentsu. Naturally, I couldn't pass up such an opportunity.

I had been planning to acquire a facsimile machine for quite some time to send and receive copy and design over a phone line. This would save a tremendous amount of my time since the preliminary designs and corrections could be handled without my having to run them around. This was the perfect opportunity for me to test one out. I purchased one and was shocked with the superb quality of the images. The machine also reported the place that documents were sent as well as the date, time, and how long it took for transmission. It was amazing. I could service clients anywhere with the telephone being the only necessary piece of equipment for transaction. Before long I was able to send 12 designs to Mr. Inagaki.

1 Photo used for annual report cover in Japanese.
2 Removable sign on a stand to announce morning service.
3 The logo applied to a modern building in a downtown area.
4 McDonald's in Japanese and Royal Host in English on the same billboard.
5 The Royal Host logo applied to an East Coast cottage-style shop.

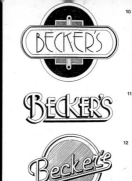

1　　2　　3　　4　　5

6　　7　　8　　9　　10

soon realized that using the facsimile machine also had its pitfalls. The process is so fast that they had a tendency to jump to conclusions without giving the proposals proper consideration. Mr. Inagaki, an excellent and experienced designer himself, said six of the nine designs I originally submitted would not work in Japan. However, two of the original six survived Royal's evaluation and the final design was chosen from one of them.

The most important element in design for this project was to come up with a logo superior to McDonald's. The famous golden arch is immediately recognizable and is nostalgic for those who grew up in the 50s. The "M" design is unique, but from a design viewpoint, not very creative. However, I got the feeling that the management of Royal believed that the success of McDonald's had a lot to do with just the logo design itself. So I based my plan on this theory.

I visited the McDonald's museum in Des Plaines, Illinois to find out how the golden arch logo evolved. This museum is an "original" McDonald's restaurant that has been restored and displays McDonald's memorabilia. Sure enough, I found a progressive change in the logo over the years. When I presented my three final designs to Royal, I also submitted slides which showed the history of the McDonald's logo.

The final design is similar to Royal Host's logo, although it incorporates shadows and the type weight is heavier. The other two final designs were interesting, but did not have that "family" resemblance for quick recognition.

Royal plans to build only 15 stores in three years. They would like to thoroughly test the system and bring it to perfection before they offer a franchise. I hope to continue working with Mr. Makoto Kitaguchi, director of marketing, to make the chain not only better than McDonald's, but the best in the world.

1-3 *Nine designs in rough form were sent by FAX as an initial proposal to find the direction.*

4-6 *Another nine trials with different styles were submitted in the second phase.*

7-10 *Eleven more logos were added.*

11-13 *The final presentation of three designs. Photo #13 was chosen as the official logo by the management.*

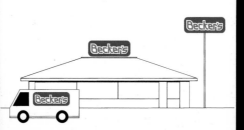
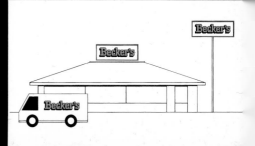

ILLINOIS CPA SOCIETY

This organization is for certified public accountants who practice within the State of Illinois. It aims to build better relations among members and acquaint them with new laws and technology through ongoing seminars, classes and conventions.

Ellen Farnsworth, who was with another company I had done some work for in the past, had moved to the Illinois CPA Society and brought me in. I have learned that in the U.S., people do not stay in one job for long periods of time. This helps me out because if they liked my work in one business, they may call me once they move onto another. That is what happened in this and in many other cases, thus expanding my work in many areas.

I designed a number of brochures, schedules and internal communication pieces for this society. Mark Weiting, the director of communications, was very understanding toward creative design, having been an artist himself.

One of the most difficult things to do in graphic design is to make a schedule of events both readable and easily understood. I designed a schedule divided by time zones to avoid confusion when attendees had a choice of many programs taking place simultaneously.

Now, most of the production work, including typesetting, is done internally at the Illinois CPA Society. Many of their publications are computerized, thus eliminating the need for outside assistance.

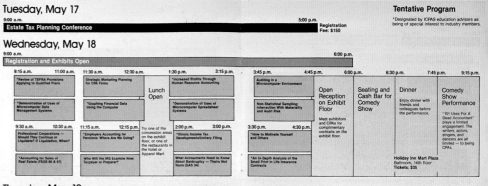

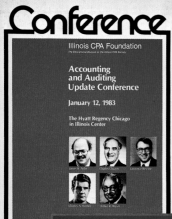

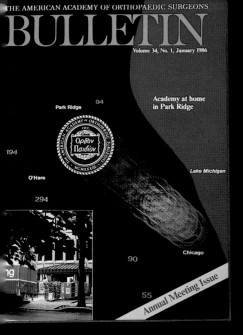

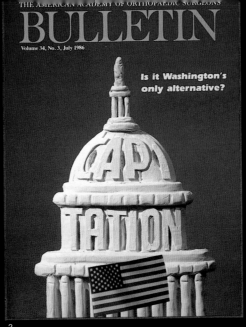

to Park Ridge.

2 *Capitation (same medical fee for everyone) was superimposed on a U.S. Capital Building.*

3 *The writing on the cast tells the complex story of the industry's conflicting problems.*

4 *Compliments are simple, added pleasures to my job as an artist.*

5 *The existing logo for the American Academy of Orthopaedic Surgeons (left), and new logo (yet to be proposed).*

AMERICAN ACADEMY OF ORTHOPAEDIC SURGEONS

ark Weiting called. Not from the Illinois CPA ociety, but from the American Academy of rthopaedic Surgeons where he took a osition as Communications Director.

he Academy, representing 13,000 bone octors throughout the U.S., had just moved om downtown Chicago to Park Ridge in the orthern suburbs. They needed a cover esign for the next issue of their magazine epicting the move.

Since Park Ridge is not necessarily well-known to Academy members or clients, we needed a reference to major highways and O'Hare airport, so we started out with a map.

I constructed a three-dimensional map with grey paper and superimposed the Academy's logo moving from Chicago to Park Ridge with a rainbow-colored tail. This photographic technique was invented by me 15 years ago, and I have yet to see anyone else use it. It is not done by a computer, but is purely optical. You just move the image with different color gels and expose them on film several times.

Everyone liked the first cover design, but the next cover I was assigned to do for the Academy was more difficult. They wanted the cover to show all the turmoil the industry is facing with medical expenses, lawsuits, labor laws and liability insurance, to name a few. The concept I worked with on this assignment was based on the supposition that I broke a bone and had to wear a cast. What, I thought, would each individual involved with conflicting interests write on it? Mark and Bill Spelbring supplied the words and I supplied the cast made from my foot.

One of the pleasures of working in this country is that people don't hesitate to compliment my work, privately or officially. Not just Mark and Bill, but the *Ragan Report*, a monthly news report of communications, appreciated and acknowledged my work. Even a division of the government requested copies of this issue.

I designed a new logo for the Academy that I have not proposed yet. I want to see Mark and Bill's reaction when they see this page.

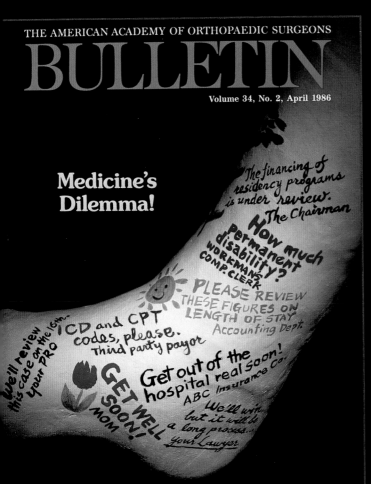

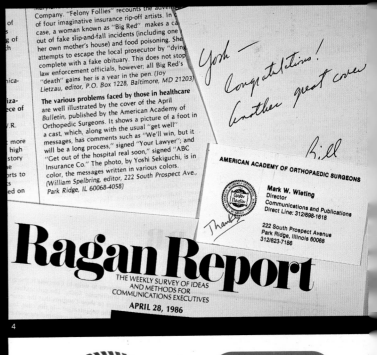

U.S. LEAGUE OF SAVINGS INSTITUTIONS

In the United States, there are two places you can put your money: banks and savings and loan institutions. They both provide similar services. They're very similar although banks invest more in businesses and foreign countries while S & Ls loan funds to individuals for things such as home mortgages.

The U.S. League of Savings Institutions is a 93 year-old association with a membership of 3,500. Its members hold more than 93% of the nation's $1 trillion in savings institutions assets. The League provides a full range of services to its members including technical guidance, legislative and regulatory information, meetings that provide both information and business contacts, and a host of informative publications.

Nancy Hicks from SRDS introduced me to the association. The editors I worked with on League projects were Nancy Lapp and Bill Marshall.

There are very strict rules governing the application of the League logo to various media. The logotype and a chevron have to be used exactly as they are. Colors and angles of the chevron cannot be altered, and every design proposal is examined and approved by their law department.

The Savings Institutions Sourcebook, one of the League's key publications, provides basic information and detailed data. When I design the cover each year, I propose a number of design approaches for them to choose from.

A design is selected not only because of good graphics but also because it reflects the cover price of the books. For example, a design may work for a textbook-type publication but would not be appropriate for a hardbound, more expensive book.

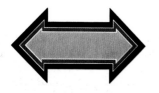

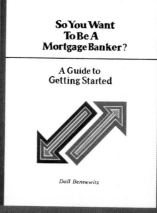

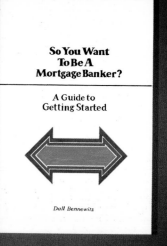

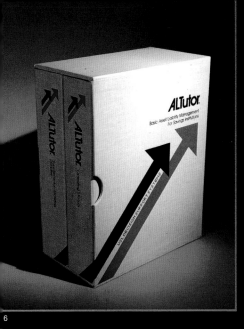

6

7

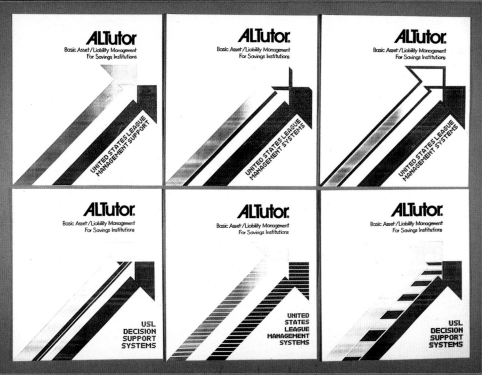

8

1 *The 1986 edition of the Savings Institutions Sourcebook. Using a chevron, I gave the "86" a three-dimensional look.*

2 *A proposal for the "86" (right) to follow a design used two years before.*

3 *Another proposed design for 1986. I try to give each proposal a different look.*

4 *Book cover for mortgage bankers.*

5 *Of these three proposals, the one on the right was selected.*

6-7 *A newly published set of computer disks and books.*

8 *Numerous variations of the chevron were carefully evaluated by the law department. The originals were in black, red and blue.*

9 *A four-color printing process was used for the "Human Resources Management" book. This book also contained a number of charts.*

10 *This newsletter design is for the office in Washington, D.C. The capitol building adds a hint of authority.*

11 *Three proposals. The originals were red and blue. (FDIC is misspelled in one of them . . . nobody's perfect).*

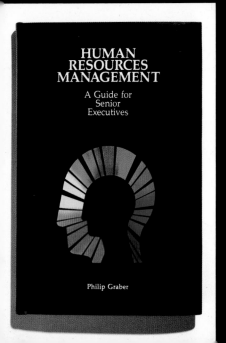

11

ENJOY EUROPE IN YOUR OWN MERCEDES-bENZ

MERCEDES-BENZ

The poster above was made by using a photograph I took on a family trip to Europe in 1966. It is in the open market area in the ancient city of Rothenberg, at the top of Romantiche Straase. I superimposed a picture in the logo with copy reading, "Enjoy Europe in your own Mercedes-Benz." I was told later that the traffic sign in the picture indicated a "No Parking Zone."

This example clearly reveals my design philosophy. If I remove one element, the poster loses its function. This poster was used by an Illinois dealership to promote M-B's European Delivery Plan.

Because their three-pointed star symbol resembles a peace symbol used widely in the 60s, I designed a speculative poster for the company adding just a line to their mark as if the poster were slightly marred by graffitti to pray for peace in the holiday season. M-B rejected this concept on the basis that the war in Vietnam was being criticized and the peace symbol was directly associated to hippies and flower children. (Oops! Here I even managed to misspell America).

peace!

Seasons Greetings from
Mercedes-Benz of North Ameica

FIRESTONE TIRE

Firestone makes heavy duty tires for specific industrial uses as well as for the consumer market. Some tires they manufacture are as tall as a three-story building.

The first time we started a series of ads for the industrial tires, we planned to create one ad for each specific application. We created a slogan "Moving the World . . . with the Right Tires for the Right Job," and formed the shape of a tire with segments of photographs, which would be used in their entirety later on.

Firestone's experience and expertise are moving the world with tires designed for every job that needs to get done. And we'll help you select the right tire for *your* job saving down time and money and providing longer wear. We'll even bring our expertise directly to you with on-site seminars designed to assess

your needs and solve your problems. Whether your job is construction or mining or forestry or farming, Firestone has the right tire for the right job. So, go with Firestone and keep *your* world moving.

Firestone
INTERNATIONAL COMPANY
1200 Firestone Parkway, Akron, Ohio 44317 U.S.A.

It Takes A Tough Tire... In *Your* Rugged World

Firestone's experience and expertise are moving the world with the right tire for the right job. Our Forestry Special is built to meet the demanding needs of the logging industry. Two steel tread plies under the tread provide excellent resistance to impact, puncture, and snag even under the most rugged conditions. Wide traction bars

with wide bases and full shoulder-to-shoulder contact provide continuous traction. The right tire for the right job means longer wear and less down time. So, go with Firestone and keep *your* world moving.

Firestone
INTERNATIONAL COMPANY
1200 Firestone Parkway, Akron, Ohio 44317 U.S.A.

The second ad for the series, shown above, is for logging tractors. Ron Arnold, a photographer/environmentalist who used to contribute articles to *Logging Management* magazine, a Vance publication, took the photos. Unfortunately, *Logging* is no longer published. They were shot in the State of Washington, where a lot of U.S. logging takes place. It is often through contacts that I make by working in one industry that I can accomplish design ideas for another. Nadine Richterman wrote the copy.

Los Angeles: City in the Sun

Plymouth | **TRAVELER**
YOUR COMPLETE TOUR GUIDE | VOLUME VI/NUMBER 5

PLYMOUTH TRAVELER

This publication, edited and published by Medalist Publications under the supervision of Chrysler Corporation, stemmed from a public relations and promotion campaign for Plymouth car owners. The book covered a number of U.S. cities giving the reader information on vacation travel. We tried to come up with a theme for each city covered, recreating the atmosphere of that particular city. For example, in order to express bright, sunny Los Angeles (this was before Los Angeles became known for its smog), I used colorful tissue paper to make a collage. I then made brush drawings, overprinting the tissue art.

This book was designed by Dick Helland and edited by Jim Ward. I did the illustrations.

GAS RESEARCH INSTITUTE

This institute awards funds to organizations researching new and more efficient means of developing gas energy sources. In an effort to raise awareness of the importance of gas as a source of energy, it publishes educational and informational literature.

An annual international convention is attended by many foreign delegates. Therefore, the convention pamphlet, containing detailed program information for each session, is very important. Jerry Long, the director of communications, allowed me to design this piece without limitations on design or printing cost.

HEWLETT-PACKARD

This area is now called Silicon Valley, but when I was there in 1967, it was just a sleepy town at the foot of a mountain range separating Palo Alto from the Pacific coast. This is where Hewlett-Packard, one of the oldest companies in the computer and electronics industry, is situated.

I was freelancing for an agency in the city. One day a comp layout designed by a senior art director was rejected and returned. An account executive let me give it a try as a last resort. I whipped it up in one day and they approved it. It made me uncomfortable to see the look on the art director's face, but perhaps my straightforward approach without any gimmicks was what the company management was looking for.

CNA INSURANCE

I worked at CNA after I left Medalist. Soon after I started, I noticed my feelings sinking by the day. I analyzed it and concluded it was the job. Many of the brochures I designed carried headlines such as: "You have a 25% chance of getting cancer by the age of 60," and "During one year, 3% of children are involved in traffic accidents." These everyday statistics were getting to me.

Before I was totally discouraged, OSHA (Occupational Safety and Health Administration) was created and I was assigned to design a brochure. It was a departure from the routine and I chose Uncle Sam as the spokesman, using a lighthearted cartoon illustration. Red and blue were overprinted on black line illustrations. It was like a breath of fresh air!

AT&T

I make a lot of international phone calls from Chicago to Japan. A big problem I used to face was the 15 hour time difference and having to figure out what time and day it would be in Japan before I could make a phone call. I made a map of time zones that enabled me to immediately find out what time it was in any city all over the world when matched with a certain hour of the day in Chicago. I wanted to share my invention with others facing the same problem, so I wrote AT&T to see if they could use it. Unfortunately, they already had a similar device in the form of a sliding scale made to fit in an envelope. It was slightly more difficult to use, but considering size versus function, I'd say our inventions were a tie.

MIDWEST BUDDHIST TEMPLE

This temple, located in Chicago, is a sect of Jyodo-Shinshu, which follows the teachings of Koubou-Daishi, the same teachings my ancestors followed. Since Noby Yamakoshi of Nobart, Inc. belonged to the temple, I had the opportunity to design literature for them.

Japanese people, including myself, are not very religious. Every house has a Butsudan, or small temple and Kamidana, or Shinto-shrine on a shelf. Young people have wedding ceremonies in Christian churches and are buried in Buddhist cemeteries. Japanese Americans who are Buddhist do not send Christmas cards and they keep the Japanese traditions for the New Year.

When I joined Nobart, the new temple was just planned and my first design job was a brochure for the new temple. I tried to show the beauty of Japan so I made brush paintings. Other assignments included making invitations and programs for a concert, Thanksgiving and New Year greeting cards, seals and posters.

I never knew that Buddhist hymns existed and never dreamed of writing Sutra in Japanese in the land of Yankees!

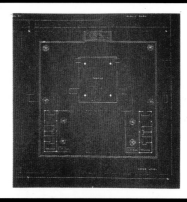

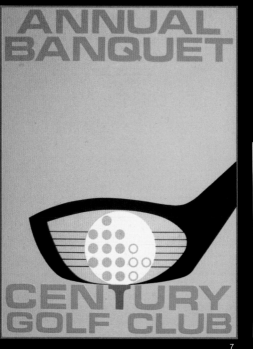

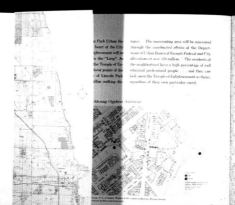

You're invited...

8

You're invited to attend the 2nd Annual MBC Choir Concert

Date: Saturday, March 19, 1966
Time: 8:00 P.M.
Place: MBC chapel
1763 N. North Park Ave.
Chicago, Ill.

Hear Buddhist Gathas, Folk and Popular Songs

- MBC Choir
- MBC Male Choir
- MBC-BTC Combined Choir
- Special Guest Performance
  Marc Gordon
  Diane Kayano

Light Refreshments Served

2nd Annual MBC Choir Concert

Saturday, March 19, 1966
8:00 P.M.
MBC chapel
1763 N. North Park Ave.
Chicago, Ill.

10

The brochure for the newly planned Midwest Buddhist Temple. Sutra in Japanese characters are shown on the inside front and back pages. The Sumie brush paintings were incorporated inside to emphasize Japanese beauty.

7　Poster for the Century Golf Club banquet. Century refers to golfers who shoot around 100, like me.

8-9　An invitation for the annual concert using a wood-cut to depict heavenly musicians.

10　The concert program with gatefold cover.

11　An inside look at the program. Among the popular American songs sung by choirs, I sang "Cool Water," an all-time western classic.

12　A seal to commemorate Bodhi Day, when young Buddha obtained enlightenment under the bodhi tree.

13　A New Year's greeting card for our friends Rich and Ruth Kaneko and their son.

14　A Thanksgiving card sent along with gifts to Nobart's clients.

12

PROGRAM

Conductor: Rev. Yukei Ashikaga
Assistant Conductor: Ray Kayano
Pianists: Amy Katahira
Ruth Kaneko

I Buddhist Gathas (Sangoka)
1. "Wazawai No" (Ominous Dark Cloud) .... Kozaburo Hirai
2. "Mihotoke Wa" (Amitabha, Oneness of Life) .... Kiyoshi Nobutoki
   Soloist, Alice Yamamoto
3. "Aokusa Wa" (Green Grass) .... Yuji Koseki
   Soloist, Kay Arima

II Buddhist Gathas (Sangoka)
1. "Otera No Ishidan" (Stairway to the Temple) .... Yoshinao Nakata
2. "Sakiniou" (Wafting Fragrance) .... Kozaburo Hirai
   Soloist, Kaz Fujishima
3. "Kokoro No Wagaya" (True Abode of my Heart) .... Masao Koga
   Soloist, Tosh Nishimura
4. "Hotokesama Wa" (Where the Buddha is) .... Ryutaro Hirota

III Guest Performance by the Buddhist Temple of Chicago Choir
   Conductor: Rev. Yukei Ashikaga   Pianist: Ruth Kumata
1. "Hokekyosan" (The Song in Praising the Sutra Hokekyo) ... K. Yoshikawa
2. "Midori No Oniwa" (The Garden Green) .... Yoshinao Nakata
3. "Mina Wo Tonaen" (Yearning Profound) .... Kunio Toda

INTERMISSION

IV Guest Artists, Diane Kayano and Marc Gordon
1. Sonata in G Minor .... G. Ph. Telemann
   Oboe, Marc Gordon; Accompanist, Diane Kayano
2. Sonate (For two Flutes) .... J. Ch. Naudot

V Choral selections from "The Sound of Music".......... Rodgers and Hammerstein
1. The Sound of Music
2. My Favorite Things
3. Do Re Mi

VI MBC Male Choral Group
1. Cool Water .... Bob Nolan
   Soloist, Yoshi Sekiguchi
2. You'll Never Walk Alone .... Rodgers and Hammerstein

VII MBC and BTC Combined Choir
1. "Oyedo Nihonbashi" (Tokyo District Folk Song)
2. "Minegumi No" (Radiant Compassion) .... Yuji Koseki

PROGRAM NOTES

The SANGOKA—Song of Praise of the Buddha
Immediately following the end of World War II, the Abbot and Lady Kocho Otani of the Higashi Honganji of Kyoto, Japan, realizing the material and spiritual devastation caused by the war, decided to revive Buddhism through music. They asked that poems be submitted to them which could be set to music. Selected poems were arranged for singing by several famous Japanese composers. During this time Abbot Otani organized the Otani Gakuen Choir which has since become one of the important choral groups in Japan. The MBC Choir are presenting a few of the selections.

GUEST ARTISTS

MARC GORDON, now a senior at Senn High School, began studying the oboe during his freshman year. He is a student of Mr. Richard Kanter, who is an oboist with the Chicago Symphony Orchestra. With hopes of a career in music, Marc will continue his studies at Roosevelt University.
In the past, Marc has been a member of the Chicago All-City Band. He has also performed with Roosevelt University's Concert Band and the Chicago Sinfonietta. In the summer of 1965, he won a scholarship to the famous Interlochen Music Camp in Michigan. Presently the principal oboist in Senn's concert band and orchestra, Marc is also a member of the Youth Orchestra of Chicago, and the Civic Orchestra of Chicago. His most recent achievement is having received a highly superior rating in the Instrumental Solo Competition of Chicago Public High Schools.

DIANE KAYANO is a sophomore at Mundelein College. She, too, began studying the oboe while at Senn High School. Although she is not a music major, Diane continues to play the oboe as an extra-curricular activity. Her teacher is Mr. Jerry Sirucek, a former member of the Chicago Symphony Orchestra, who is now teaching at Indiana University.
Diane's past experiences include the Chicago All-City Band, and the Concert Band at Roosevelt University. She is presently solo oboist with the Chicago Sinfonietta, and a member of the Chamber Players at Mundelein College.

CONDUCTOR'S PROFILE

REV. YUKEI ASHIKAGA became a member of the Otani University Male Chorus in 1948. Since that time he has conducted and managed, as well as sung, with several choral groups. In 1953, he organized the Linden Male Chorus composed of graduates of the Otani University Male Chorus. During 1953 to 1958, he served in three capacities: as conductor of the Otani High School Male Chorus and the Tree-Peony Choir (Otani Gakuen Junior Choir) and as manager of the Otani Gakuen Choir, one of the most distinguished choral groups in Japan. In 1959, he arrived in Chicago and organized the BTC Choir. Shortly thereafter, he was assigned as assistant minister to the Buddhist Temple of Chicago. Through his inspirational leadership and ability in music, he was requested by the Midwest Buddhist Church to organize and conduct their choir group in November, 1961.

11

迎春

一九六六年元旦

金子　忍

繁　淑子

Shō Chiku Bai (Pine-Bamboo-Plum)
Symbolizes Perpetual Youth, Vitality and Perseverance.

Health, Happiness
and Prosperity
for 1966

rich, ruth and jeff
kaneko

Our Thanks
to You . . .

In 1965, We are Thankful . . .
For all the things in our society
in which we live
For the health, liberty and
the pursuit of happiness
and above all
For your friendship and good will
that we treasure

Nobart, inc.

JEWISH COMMUNITY CENTERS OF CHICAGO

Judaism is the origin of many religions, including Christianity. There are a dozen or so places in Chicago where Jewish-Americans meet to gather donations to send to Israel and to participate in other activities such as helping the elderly and needy in the Jewish community.

I am not a prejudiced man. In fact, I find it interesting to work with and learn about other people, traditions and cultures. I have designed for many different people, organizations and companies with all variations of color, religion and beliefs. From a design point of view, I didn't always agree with this client's design or color choice, but at the same time I had respect for their taste as part of their history from a cultural viewpoint.

The Jewish people are strongly opinionated, which is neither good or bad, but is contrary to Japanese behavior and upbringing. Therefore, I was very diplomatic in presenting my work. I designed a brochure to recruit volunteers in helping the needy as well as a calendar of events for this organization.

1 *The brochure used to recruit volunteers contained a conveniently placed reply card so it only needed to be cut on one side. This color combination was among the client's favorite.*

2-3 *The calendar of events included illustrated highlights for each month. Some research was necessary for me to understand the history and culture of the Jewish origin.*

1

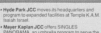

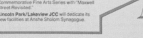
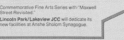

1

IDEAL

This company is located in the western part of Illinois near the Mississippi River. It is a large manufacturer of electrical products that are used mainly for wiring. These products are exported to countries around the world.

I was assigned to develop this company's first corporate advertisement. I tried to come up with the most powerful way to show the scope of their export business. After I discovered that 80 countries received their products, I came up with the idea of spelling out the company name with 80 national flags. This concept proved to be flexible for use in different applications as well as for use in publications from all of the countries involved.

1 *The design concept in final form, using 80 national flags to spell out the company name. Note the Rising Sun flag upfront.*

2 *For product ads, I applied the same design concept using the flags for a border.*

3-5 *The same corporate ad is shown here in three different tongues. These ads appeared in magazines all over the world.*

Nadene Richterman was the copywriter for these ads.

2

It Takes 80 Flags To Spell Our Name

And in each of these 80 countries, Ideal promises greater value for your money. Our Ideal philosophy has been around for over 65 years: every Ideal electrical product gives more value in terms of service than the money you pay. Ideal's professional experience in the development and manufacture of electrical tools, equipment, and supplies means quality plus value ...in over 3600 different products....products like IDEAL PRECISION WIRE STRIPPERS for industrial use...or IDEAL

FISH-TAPE and YELLOW 77® WIRE PULLING LUBRICANT for quicker easier wire pulling ...or IDEAL ABRASIVES, GRINDERS, and RESURFACING STONES for commutator maintenance. Ideal products promise dependability and ease...saving you time and money. So, wherever you are...whatever you need... whenever you want quality, make it Ideal. Our name spells quality plus value...under 80 flags around the world.

IDEAL

IDEAL INDUSTRIES, INC.
Export Department
Becker Place, Sycamore, IL 60178 U.S.A.

راية «آيديل» ترفرف على ثمانين دولة
كل منها ينطق اسمنا

«آيديل» تعادل بضاعة أموالك، ذلك في كل دولة من الدول الثمانين التي تمد لها خدماتنا. ان فلسفة «آيديل» والتي يقدر عمرها بما يزيد عن ٦٥ عاماً مبارة عن: جميع أجهزة «آيديل» الكهربائية تعطيك قيمة أكثر من أموالك. وذلك في الخدمة التي تقدمها لك. ان خبرة «آيديل» المتخصصة في انتاج وتطوير الأجهزة والمعدات الكهربائية، تعني النوعية والجودة .... وذلك بين أكثر من ٣٦٠٠ صنف، وهي مبارة عن: الاسلاك الكهربائية باللينة المتطورة، والتي تستخدم في مجال الصناعة، كذلك «فيش تيب و يلو ٧٧ (R)» والتي «Fish - Tape and Yellow 77 (R)» تمتاز بسرعة وسهولة التركيب، كما تجعل عملية السحب سهلة للغاية.

«آيديل» تعني النوعية والجودة ... اطلب «آيديل».

IDEAL

IDEAL INDUSTRIES, INC.
Export Department
Becker Place, Sycamore, IL 60178 U.S.A.

Se necesitan 80 banderas para deletrear nuestro nombre

Y en cada uno de estos 80 países, Ideal promete más provecho por su dinero. Nuestra filosofía Ideal está en el mercado desde hace más de 65 años: cada producto eléctrico Ideal es más valioso en función del servicio que proporciona que el dinero que pagó Ud. por él. La experiencia profesional de Ideal en el desarrollo y fabricación de herramientas eléctricas, equipo, y suministros significa calidad más valor...en más de 3.600 productos...productos como los DESOLLADORES DE CABLES IDEAL DE PRECISION para uso industrial ...o la CINTA PARA PESCAR

CABLES y el LUBRICANTE YELLOW 77™ DE ARRASTRE IDEAL, para sacar alambres eléctricos con rapidez y facilidad...o las PIEDRAS ABRASIVAS, AMOLADORAS, y RECTIFICADORAS IDEAL para mantenimiento de conmutadores. Los productos Ideal le prometen confiabilidad y sencillez...ahorrándole tiempo y dinero. O sea que, donde quiera que este...lo que sea que necesite...siempre que desee calidad: busque Ideal. Nuestro nombre quiere decir calidad más valor...bajo 80 banderas alrededor del mundo.

IDEAL

IDEAL INDUSTRIES, INC.
Export Department
Becker Place, Sycamore, IL 60178 U.S.A.

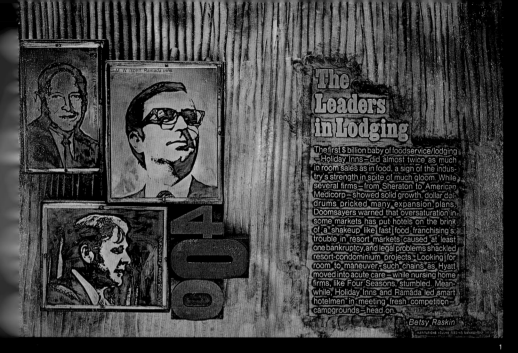

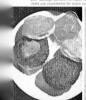

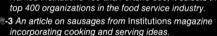

Magazines published in the U.S. are roughly divided into two groups: business and consumer. The major difference is that the former are usually distributed without charge to targeted audiences made up of professional groups of people and the latter are sold through subscription or on newsstands and are available to the common folk.

Most of the magazines I have designed for are business publications, so if you are not in the same professional fields that they are aimed at then you probably haven't ever seen my work.

Business publications are financed through advertising revenue, so keeping a ratio between ads and editorial pages is important in order for the publication to be profitable. The usual ratio is 60% advertising to 40% editorial.

The main reason for targeted business magazines is quite obvious: It is easier for advertisers to reach the market they are interested in promoting their products or services to. For example, if you manufacture sausage you could find a business publication targeted to reach hotels, restaurants and other "mass-feeding" institutions or you could pay the high cost of advertising to the public through consumer magazines for individual sales.

Institutions magazine, now called *Restaurants and Institutions*, is the largest business publication in the food service industry. The magazine is published twice a month with a circulation of 100,000. Because each issue contains approximately 300 pages, I was working on daily deadlines when I was art director of this publication in 1970.

Aside from regular articles on food service news and information, we also featured problems associated with feeding the elderly. Dave Hanks wrote the copy.

Named Institutions 400 à la Fortune 500, it selects the top 400 organizations in the food service industry.

-3 An article on sausages from Institutions magazine incorporating cooking and serving ideas.

Ad revenue is important to the livelihood of the business magazine. These publications often solicit for advertising that can be tied in with a feature article. Here, ad pages for Oscar Mayer are incorporated.

-12 The welfare of the elderly is becoming an increasing problem throughout the world. Here, we tackled the many methods of feeding them to keep good health. Testimonials were set in large type and appeared inside the picture area. The man in picture #7 is saying "I'm 107 and can out-dance anyone here," and the woman in picture #8 is muttering, "Being old isn't a crime, but it isn't a joy."

5

young at heart

6

young
at heart

"I'm 107 and I can
still out-dance
anyone here."

7

FROM RESTAURANTS TO SCHOOLS
Age Brings Opportunity

"Being old isn't
a crime, but it
isn't a joy."

8

FROM RESTAURANTS TO SCHOOLS
Age Brings Opportunity

MANNING'S SENIOR PLATE MENU

SUNDAY	TOMATO POT ROAST
MONDAY	HAM STEAK
TUESDAY	HAMBURGER PATTY
WEDNESDAY	FISH CAKES
THURSDAY	FRIED CHICKEN LIVERS
FRIDAY	BAKED COD
SATURDAY	TOMATO MEAT LOAF
	MIXED GREEN SALAD
	MASHED POTATOES
	VEGETABLE
	JELLO or PUDDING
	COFFEE or TEA

"My birthday party
was real nice-
felt like a lord."

9

MEALS ON WHEELS
For Seniors Who Live at Home

"They really look forward
to my visit.
You can see it."

10

RETIREMENT HOMES
Food, Shelter, A Social Experience

"Some things get better.
I can handle a cue
as sure as anyone."

CHELSEA HOUSE
Ethnic Day dinner
FESTA DI ITALIANO

11

RETIREMENT HOMES
A Social Experience

SENIOR
CITIZENS
NEWS

NURSING HOMES
Where Food Spells Success

12

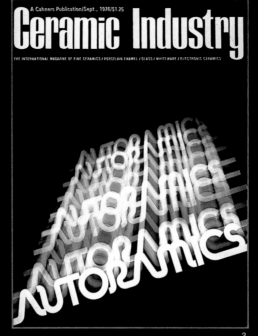

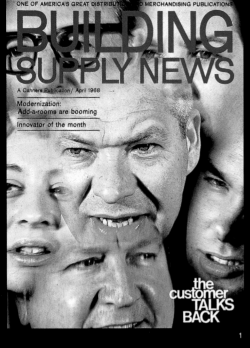

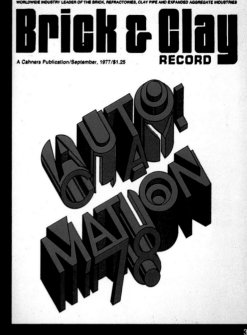

BUILDING SUPPLY NEWS

This magazine, a Cahners publication, is geared toward the building material industry. It has two sister publications, *Brick & Clay* and *Ceramic Industry*. I once handled all three of these publications myself. Having less than 10 working days to allocate to each and meet overlapping publishing dates was an incredible experience! I gained a lot of confidence in myself and I realized that nothing is impossible as long as I am determined enough to accomplish it.

1 *"The customer talks back." I used a six-faceted prism lens and by covering five facets and recording one image at a time, I achieved six angry faces on one film.*

2 *When suitable photos were not available, I resorted to typography to get the point across. Here I used type on a vertical screen and changed the color of the back-lighting lamp while moving away from the camera.*

3 *I chose a three-dimensional graphic for "Auto Claymation '78."*

4 *This cover depicts the process of product exposure from a trade show to consumers through hardware retailers.*

5 *A maze constructed with thick paper in the shape of a dollar sign illustrates the difficulties in marketing to reach a profit.*

6 *This illustration was used for a feature article on customers walking away without buying anything. I took instant photographs for reference.*

7 *Focus on tomorrow's market was shot with a zoom lens.*

8 *"Crack open the hardware market". The headline here was cracked using a hammer to stress the cover theme.*

9 *An award-winning cover for a section of Brick & Clay magazine entitled, "Refractories blast-off for the 70's." Here I used moving type to illustrate the blast-off. This design won the Jesse Neal Award.*

10 *The title here was constructed using the same treatment as in photo #2. The conveyer- belt style, expressing automation, was achieved by multi-exposing on the film while changing lighting color.*

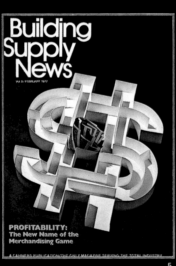

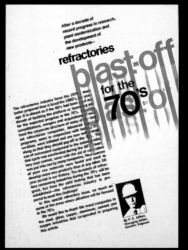

UNPUBLISHED ILLUSTRATIONS

When people ask me what I do for a living, I tell them that I am a graphic designer. Yet, the word "design" has a much broader definition than most designers think. Photography is design, using the mediums of both lens and film; and illustration is design, using a painting medium on paper.

So, when I hear someone say, "I am a photographer" or "I am an illustrator," it makes me think that they are limiting themselves to very small, specific areas of design. To me, design is a combination of all these things.

Here, I have gathered unpublished and experimental illustrations that I think are unique in style. Most illustrations I see can be divided into around ten styles and I can almost immediately determine which famous illustrator's style was imitated. It is quite all right to use someone else's technique, but I believe you should project yourself into your illustrations. Otherwise they are simply imitations, not creations.

1 The Batik technique (fabric dying method using wax and color dye) was experimented on Japanese rice paper for an illustration for the children's book "Hansel and Gretel".

2 A portrait of John F. Kennedy on Japanese handmade textured paper with fibers showing.

3 A 3-D illustration. A deck chair in the shape of Marilyn Monroe to be used for a story entitled "Comfortable Woman."

4 Using the Batik method on paper, I made the cracks deeper to express the madness of Adolph Hitler.

5 A portrait of Brigitte Bardot made up with squares filled with lines.

6-7 A series of World War I fighter planes.

8 A series of books similar to my paper car project in planning. Here, well-known WW II fighter planes are zooming over an airfield. Instead of giving the planes a hint of motion, I gave the runway an illusion of high speed.

9 A trial illustration for Joan Baez's record.

PROFESSIONAL BUILDER

Yet another magazine from Cahners Publishing Company. The art director was Dick Helland, and we often traveled together all over the country to photograph residential and apartment developments.

Dick was very attentive to detail, arranging props and moving furniture as well as camera angles. I learned a lot from working with him. He is now a vice president at Frankel and Co., Chicago, and one of his major clients is McDonald's.

Many photographs from builders and developers were submitted to the magazine for publication. They were all superb photos taken by real pros, but none of them were usable for the cover. Cover photos have to be uncluttered at the top and bottom so that the masthead and coverlines can be incorporated. When viewed without typography, cover photos usually look rather empty.

Other than architecture, I also photographed influential people in the building industry. I always tried to capture their inner quality. When you take photographs, your instinct tells you to position your camera at eye-level, but in order to get the unusual shots, the first thing I do is move the camera's position from eye-level to create a more dramatic effect.

1-6 Architectural photography from all over the country was used for cover shots (except photo #6).

7 Two cover examples, the left is from Atlanta, the right from Cape Cod.

8-10 A feature section to follow the nation's building trend. I tried to capture the geometric drama by shooting from different angles.

11-14 Portraits of trend-setters in the building industry. A good portrait should express a person's character, philosophy of life and atmosphere around him. Did I succeed?

PROFESSIONAL BUILDER

interior volumes

Involve with structural line

connect with old traditions

The Corporate Builder

The Land Wizard

The Entrepreneur

The Organization Man

HOME CENTER MAGAZINE

Home Center, a Vance publication, is targeted at the home center market where consumers turn for DIY (Do-it-yourself) home improvement supplies.

When I started working for this magazine, Burt Winick, who was art director at Cahners when I worked there, was the designer. Whenever he went on vacation, I filled in for him. Burt later resigned after an argument with one of the editors and I was asked to take over. I declined at first because I had no intention of taking Burt's account. Otherwise I'd be "Onshirazu," Japanese for a person who ignores indebtedness. I finally accepted the offer because they would have had to hire someone anyway and Burt was kind enough to understand my situation.

As with other magazine covers, I designed *Home Center's* so that they would depict the feature story simply and effectively. Some of the topics were repeated year after year, making it difficult at times to come up with new and different ideas. This is why I think editorial design is much more challenging than advertising. In advertising, all ads are basically a one-shot deal and you don't have to give a lot of thought to what you have done before.

I usually only have one week for conceptualizing, designing and shooting the cover which leaves little time for goofing off.

I tried something new and unusual in designing the cover of this magazine, something that I'd never seen before in my career. It stems from my design philosophy that less is more. I put the masthead right into the photograph as if it was a part of the subject. The two covers pictured below were created this way.

I am assigned to do 12 covers a year. I often forget to compare the most recent design to past issue designs. If I used red as a dominant color on the last cover, naturally I would not want to use red on the next one. Now I try to gather 12 consecutive covers so that the cover I am designing will lend a sort of continuity without repetition.

Another careful consideration when designing magazine covers is where the mailing label will be placed. You don't want the mailing label to cover an important element of the design or type. This happens quite often without notice because people in the editorial department usually do not receive their own publications by mail. An old Japanese proverb states, "Toudai moto kurashi," or "it is darkest at the foot of a lighthouse."

1. For this issue, featuring paint and sundries, I made up a label of a paint can incorporating the masthead, thus eliminating one graphic element from the cover.
2. To illustrate the annual Home Center Show in Texas, I carved and stamped the design on a piece of leather.
3. Photography with a prism lens gives the illusion of expansion.
4. I created a game to control inventory problems. The copy was written by Jack Nerad, now with Motor Trend *magazine.*
5. This issue featured cheap imports from the Far East.
6. I incorporated cover lines within the building plans for a deck.
7. Here, I spelled "Energy" backwards on clear glass and shot a caulking gun through it so that the letters seem to float in the air.
8. Issue on lighting. My daughter Chika's hands were used as a model.
9. This is also for paint and sundries. For a different approach, I chose to shoot straight down on a group of open paint cans.
10. Here again I put the masthead on a box to represent the story of private labeling.
11. To compare the DIY market to commercial and professional markets, I adopted a graph approach. This was a departure from usual cover designs.
12. Another cover for the Home Center Show. I used a paper construction of the U.S. map incorporating the show logo.
13. The Home Center Show awards top marketers in the business. Many award-winning home centers use this widely for their promotions.
14. Paint feature again? I painted Old Glory.
15. Droplets from a faucet spell out "Kitchen & Bath."
16. I poured water into a thin flower vase to express the plumbing issue.
17. Promotions to draw a crowd . . . stamped footprints using a variety of colors.
18. The Home Center brand apron carries hardware items.

Home Center
MAGAZINE JULY/1982

Why Gee Co. Shuns Slick Look
With 'Down Home' Merchandising

Samuln on Buyer Training

Helping your Customers Fight
The Living Space Crunch

3

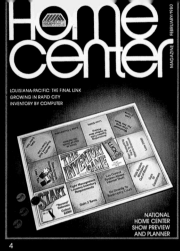

Home Center
MAGAZINE FEBRUARY/1980

LOUISIANA-PACIFIC: THE FINAL LINK
GROWING IN RAPID CITY
INVENTORY BY COMPUTER

THE INVENTORY GAME
START

NATIONAL
HOME CENTER
SHOW PREVIEW
AND PLANNER

4

Home Center
MAGAZINE FEBRUARY/1984

IMPORTS:
Why Retailers
Are Buying More

New Concrete Mix
Marketing Plans

Showcasing
255 Innovator
Award Entries

5

Home Center
MAGAZINE FEBRUARY 1984

PLANNING FOR YOUR
DIY DECK STRATEGY

First Annual INNOVATOR Awards Program

6

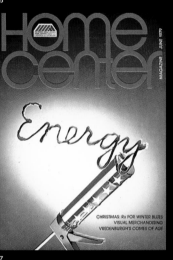

Home Center
MAGAZINE JUNE 1979

Energy

CHRISTMAS: Rx FOR WINTER BLUES
VISUAL MERCHANDISING
VREDENBURGH'S COMES OF AGE

7

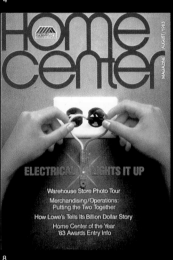

Home Center
MAGAZINE AUGUST/1983

ELECTRICAL LIGHTS IT UP

Warehouse Store Photo Tour

Merchandising/Operations:
Putting the Two Together

How Lowe's Tells Its Billion Dollar Story

Home Center of the Year
'83 Awards Entry Info

8

Home Center
MAGAZINE NOVEMBER 1981

Store Security:
Loss Prevention Ideas
That Can Save You Money

Sam's...
Ou...

Selling the DIY Painter

9

Home Center
MAGAZINE MAY 1984

PRIVATE LABELING STRATEGIES

Contents: Views on brands and private labeling by
Phil Mansfield, Hechinger; Frank Denny, Home
Centers of America; Dan Senne, Stambaugh;
Thompson; Grant Hollenbeck, The Andersons;
and Frank Szymanek, Ace Hardware Corp.

BONUS

• Furniture sales outgrow seasonal status
• A close look at 8 Innovator Award winners

10

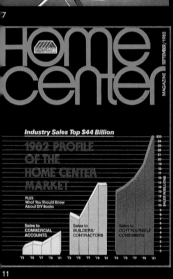

Home Center
MAGAZINE SEPTEMBER/1982

Industry Sales Top $44 Billion

1982 PROFILE
OF THE
HOME CENTER
MARKET

PLUS:
What You Should Know
About DIY Books

Sales to
COMMERCIAL
ACCOUNTS

Sales to
BUILDERS/
CONTRACTORS

Sales to
DO-IT-YOURSELF
CONSUMERS

'73 '75 '77 '79 '81

11

Home Center
MAGAZINE MARCH/1982

Where the World
Of Home Center
Retailing Meets

1982 OFFICIAL SHOW GUIDE

Plus Special Features on Computers and Competition

12

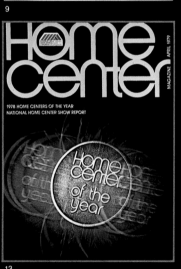

Home Center
MAGAZINE APRIL 1979

1978 HOME CENTERS OF THE YEAR
NATIONAL HOME CENTER SHOW REPORT

Home
Center
of the
year

13

Home Center
MAGAZINE NOVEMBER/1982

Paint & Decorating

• $4 Billion Business for
Home Center Retailers
• Pergament Home Centers:
East Coast Paint Power
• Kadish Profiles Stain Buyers

Four Retailers Discuss
Weathering Difficult
Business Conditions

14

Home Center
MAGAZINE MAY 1979

Major Appliances:
To Stock or Not to Stock
Home Centers Worldwide

KITCHEN & BATH

Home Center
MAGAZINE SEPTEMBER 1979

Special Report:
Advertising & Promotion

Sawyer's:
Warehouse to Home Center

DIY PLUMBING:
A Bubbling Market

Home Center
MAGAZINE OCTOBER 1982

Promotions that Keep DIYers
Beating a Path to Your Door

Planning Profits
Lawn and
Garden

Home Center
MAGAZINE

WOOD & WOOD PRODUCTS

This is a Vance publication that focuses on furniture and cabinet manufacturing. Harry Urban, a very capable young editor, and Monte Mace, publisher and a good friend of mine, give me complete freedom in design.

A big fair for the wood industry is held every other year in Los Angeles. One year, to illustrate the fair on the cover of the magazine, we used the concept of a beach scene with "L.A. Fair" reflected on a pair of sunglasses. First I tried a yellow/orange towel to reflect the California sun, but at the same time, I shot it with a blue towel, just in case this didn't work out. The unexpected result was that the blue towel caught a better, "funky" feeling of modern times.

For another issue, featuring imports from the Far East, I used an apple pie as a symbol of the American market and incorporated a hand with chopsticks digging into the pie. First, I used my youngest daughter, Juri's hand

as a model. But it didn't seem to indicate oriental labor, so I reshot it with my wife's hand and it looked more fitting. The only problem I had with this design was that the format of the cover called for the photo to be flopped, which reversed the Chinese writing on the chopsticks. Harry told me that some Taiwanese readers noticed it.

Photograph 8 on the right page has "L.A. Fair" incorporated into the famous Hollywood sign. This was Harry's concept, and we decided to use a stock photo since it was more economical than sending me out to L.A. to shoot it. Changing the name called for airbrushing out Hollywood, drawing in the background and putting new letters in. I contacted my retoucher friend and he gave me a quote that was almost three times our regular budget for the cover. I was then determined to do it myself. I didn't even have the proper equipment, but somehow I managed to finish the job in just one day. Phew!

1-3 Final cover and test shots for L.A. Fair.
4-6 Cover depicting a threat to the U.S. market from the Orient, with two test shots using different hands.
7 Reflection of an apple stresses high gloss finishing.
8 Famous Hollywood sign was replaced by the trade show's name.
9 Cover for a finishing feature. This particular photo was supplied by a manufacturer and was airbrushed on the spray area.
10 Lead page for inside section on German woodworking fair. I showed the logo separated by segments floating in the air.
11 Logo of the International Woodworking and Furniture show was projected on a white ball, giving the illusion of a planet. The stars are just small holes on a black paper, lit from behind.
12 The U.S. furniture industry is being threatened by aggressive foreign competition as illustrated by this board game.
13-17 Five covers from five different years, all about computers. It is interesting to see how they reflect their respective era.
18-20 Related magazine from Vance, Paper Trade Journal.
21 Vance's Logging Management is no longer published. This shows an example of treating catalog sections graphically.

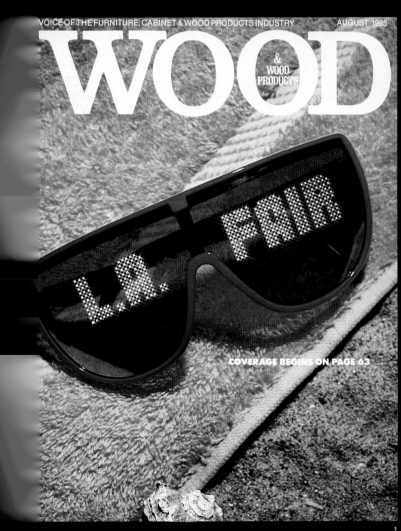

VOICE OF THE FURNITURE, CABINET & WOOD PRODUCTS INDUSTRY AUGUST 1985

WOOD
& WOOD PRODUCTS

COVERAGE BEGINS ON PAGE 63

1

VOICE OF THE FURNITURE, CABINET & WOOD PRODUCTS INDUSTRY JANUARY 1984

WOOD
& WOOD PRODUCTS

WOOD'S ANNUAL OUTLOOK SURVEY

MACHINING PARTICLEBOARD & MDF

FINISHING COLOR CONTROL PROBLEMS

WOODWORKING PRODUCTIVITY PLANS

IMPORTERS HUNGRY FOR U.S. MARKET

4

WOOD
& WOOD PRODUCTS

- YUGOSLAVIA'S SK FURNITURE
- FLAT LINE TECHNOLOGY UPDATE
- ABRASIVE & KNIFE PLANERS
- BANDSAW PROBLEMS RX

HIGH GLOSS IS IN

7

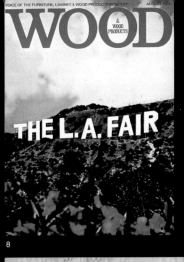

WOOD
& WOOD PRODUCTS

VOICE OF THE FURNITURE, CABINET & WOOD PRODUCTS INDUSTRY
AUGUST 1983

THE L.A. FAIR

8

WOOD
& WOOD PRODUCTS

October 1982

What's new in finishing?

- Waterborne
- Electrostatic
- Powder coating
- Clean Air Act update
- Electron beam and ultraviolet

Fastening technology review

Increasing productivity: Cutting tools

9

FOCUS ON GERMAN WOODWORKING

Preview of Ligna '85 and Interzum

Sponsored by VDMA and Wood & Wood Products

10

WOOD
& WOOD PRODUCTS

August 1982

The Louisville Fair 1982

IWF 82

Increasing productivity: Overlays & laminates

11

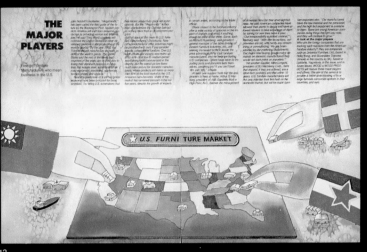

THE MAJOR PLAYERS

Foreign Furniture Manufacturers, who mean business in the U.S.

U.S. FURNITURE MARKET

12

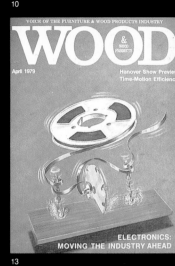

WOOD
& WOOD PRODUCTS

VOICE OF THE FURNITURE & WOOD PRODUCTS INDUSTRY

April 1979

Hanover Show Preview
Time-Motion Efficiency

ELECTRONICS: MOVING THE INDUSTRY AHEAD

13

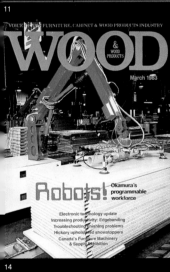

WOOD
& WOOD PRODUCTS

VOICE OF THE FURNITURE, CABINET & WOOD PRODUCTS INDUSTRY

March 1983

Robots!

Okamura's programmable workforce

Electronic technology update
Increasing productivity: Edgebanding
Troubleshooting finishing problems
Hickory upholstered showstoppers
Canada's Furniture Machinery & Supply Exhibition

14

WOOD
& WOOD PRODUCTS

VOICE OF THE FURNITURE, CABINET & WOOD PRODUCTS INDUSTRY
MARCH 1984

REVIEW OF COMPUTER-CONTROLLED MACHINERY

FOCUS ON ITALIAN WOODWORKING

GETTING THE MOST FROM YOUR MOULDER

SOLVING ASSEMBLY GLUING PROBLEMS

WHEN WILL ROBOTS MAKE FURNITURE?

15

WOOD
& WOOD PRODUCTS

VOICE OF THE FURNITURE, CABINET & WOOD PRODUCTS INDUSTRY
MARCH 1985

WHAT'S NEW IN CNC MACHINERY

DANISH FURNITURE INDUSTRY

SOLVING YOUR PEOPLE PROBLEMS

FOCUS ON WIDEBELT SANDERS

HIGH TECH IN WOODWORKING

16

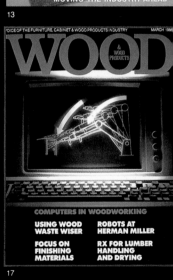

WOOD
& WOOD PRODUCTS

VOICE OF THE FURNITURE, CABINET & WOOD PRODUCTS INDUSTRY
MARCH 1986

COMPUTERS IN WOODWORKING

USING WOOD WASTE WISER

FOCUS ON FINISHING MATERIALS

ROBOTS AT HERMAN MILLER

RX FOR LUMBER HANDLING AND DRYING

17

Paper Trade Journal

- WHO'S WHO IN PAPERMAKING
- ANALYSTS VIEW WHAT'S AHEAD
- HOW TO ALIGN DIFFICULT-TO-CHECK PAPER MACHINE ROLLS
- CZ RESTRUCTURES AS GOLDSMITH WITHDRAWS
- CHESAPEAKE TO BUY MILLS FROM PHILIP MORRIS

JUNE 1985

PUBLISHED BY VANCE/WOODWORKING PUBLICATIONS

TOP 50

North America's Largest Paper Companies

50

FOCUS '84

LOGGING MANAGEMENT

FROM SEEDLING TO SAWMILL

OCTOBER 1979

- 5. Classified Buying Guide
- 4. Information Sources
- 3. Government Guide
- 2. Sawmills
- 1. Machinery & Equipment

1979 Reference Buying Guide

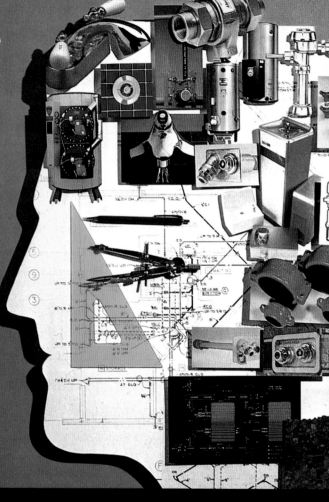

plumbing engineer

JULY/AUGUST 1984

Profile of the Plumbing Engineer

An indepth report
about who he is,
what he does,
how much money
he earns,
his age, etc.

Also:

Water Supply and Drainage Systems

Speakers Announced for ASPE Convention

1

PLUMBING ENGINEER

This magazine from Construction Industry Press is aimed at plumbing engineers, but it covers a much broader area. *Plumbing Engineer* carries technical stories on such topics as kitchen and bath layouts, fire suppression equipment, and piping for gas and liquids, boilers, heat exchangers, etc.

David Hanks, the editor of *Plumbing Engineer*, used to work with me at Medalist. We've been friends for almost 15 years.

Graphics are used on most covers so when I do use an occasional photograph, I try to make it look flat. I do not want the photographic covers to appear as a big departure from other cover treatments. Some features are difficult to illustrate. But we always came up with solutions, thanks to brainstorming sessions with John Conrad, the editorial director, and other members of the staff.

The cover on the left was designed with the best intentions but created problems for the magazine. I made up a collage with clippings of product photos from ads to portray an engineer, assuming advertisers would be glad to find their products on the cover. However, people whose products were not displayed complained about being neglected.

Next time I'll make a big foldout cover and display all the products from the book going back years. That's equality, isn't it?

1 *Profile of the plumbing engineer.*
2 Domestic Engineering *is a sister publication.*
3-4 *Redesign (right) of* HVAC Product News.
5 *To illustrate the liability insurance crisis in the industry, I showed a hand taking out the foundation of a house made out of children's blocks.*
6 *Graph expresses vacuum systems in hospitals.*
7 *Drops of water form a U.S. map.*
8 *Plumbing design for the handicapped.*
9 *Feature on medical gas piping systems.*
10 *The back-lit image was moved up and down to create the feeling of vibration.*
11 *Typograhpy treatment for a fire suppression feature.*
12 *Air brush application on colored paper for lawn irrigation story.*
13 *Cutaway view of a boiler.*

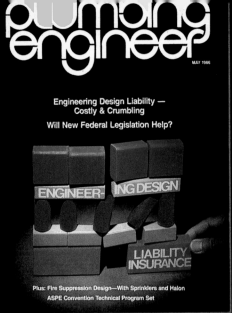

plumbing engineer

MAY 1986

Engineering Design Liability —
Costly & Crumbling

Will New Federal Legislation Help?

Plus: Fire Suppression Design—With Sprinklers and Halon

ASPE Convention Technical Program Set

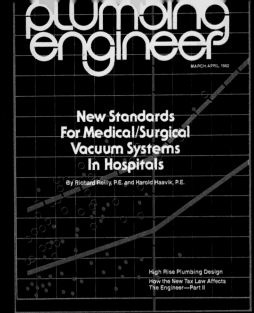

plumbing engineer

MARCH/APRIL 1982

New Standards
For Medical/Surgical
Vacuum Systems
In Hospitals

By Richard Reilly, P.E. and Harold Haavik, P.E.

High Rise Plumbing Design

How the New Tax Law Affects
The Engineer—Part II

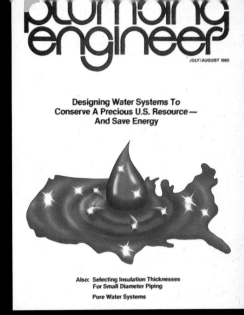

plumbing engineer

JULY/AUGUST 1986

Designing Water Systems To
Conserve A Precious U.S. Resource —
And Save Energy

Also: Selecting Insulation Thicknesses
For Small Diameter Piping

Pure Water Systems

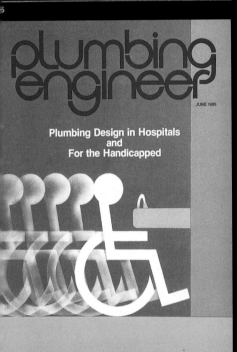

plumbing engineer

JUNE 1986

Plumbing Design in Hospitals
and
For the Handicapped

plumbing engineer

SEPTEMBER/OCTOBER 1983

Medical
Gas
Piping
Systems

By Reginald Nease P.E.

Also:

Temperature and
Relief Valves

Female Toilet Fixtures
Count Standards

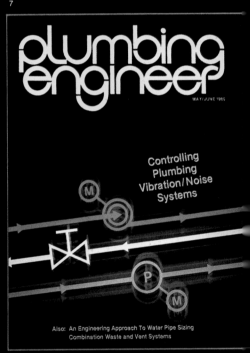

plumbing engineer

MAY/JUNE 1985

Controlling
Plumbing
Vibration/Noise
Systems

Also: An Engineering Approach To Water Pipe Sizing
Combination Waste and Vent Systems

plumbing engineer

MARCH/APRIL 1985

FIRE
SUPPRESSION

Designing
Sprinkler And Halon Systems
To Fight Fire

Also: Trends In Water Heater Selection

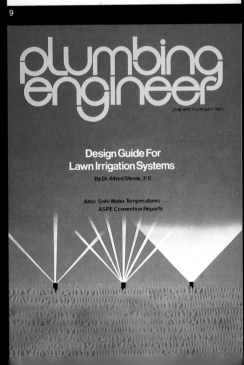

plumbing engineer

JANUARY/FEBRUARY 1985

Design Guide For
Lawn Irrigation Systems

By Dr. Alfred Steele, P.E.

Also: Safe Water Temperatures
ASPE Convention Reports

plumbing engineer

NOVEMBER/DECEMBER 1984

Effective
Heat Transfer
in Hot Water
Design

By James L. Breese

Also:

Basics of
Sound and Noise

An Interview
With New ASPE
President
Philip French

Maclean Hunter, a giant Canadian company, publishes this magazine out of its Chicago office. It covers rock products, quarry operations and cement manufacturing. *Rock Products* is edited by Dick Huhta.

A woman who used to work at Vance brought me here, although she's no longer with the company. The U.S. is a very mobile society.

This publication features an issue every year on international cement manufacturing activity. I usually treat covers with the globe in some way.

When there are no suitable photographs, I play with typography and different treatments. Sometimes I combine large type for a feature story and other contents resulting in a cover that serves as an editorial contents page.

3 Another type treatment with a rainbow-colored tail.
4 Three-dimensional setting for Forecast '85.
5 Cover with contents displayed to explain what's inside.

1

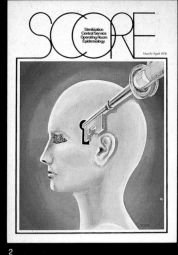

2

3

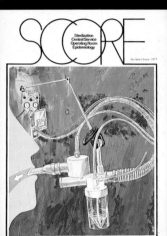

4

5

63

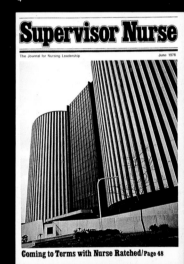

6

7

1 *Hospitals: past, present, and future.*
2 *Cover illustrating employee motivation.*
3 *The silver lining hints a feature story on positive thinking.*
4 *Respiratory equipment was drawn on a textured board.*
5 *From college to medical career, a public striptease!*
6 *Gentle and wild behavior expressed with an inkblot.*
7 *Covers for* Supervisor Nurse *used supplied photos.*

SCORE

This magazine has the longest name I've ever seen. Its official name is *Sterilization Central Service Operating Room Epidemiology*. SCORE was a PR effort from Surgicot, Inc. It ceased when the editor, Nadine Wright, passed away.

The magazine was published by S-N Publications, along with *Supervisor Nurse*, since the audience of both books coincided.

I designed the logo and cover format with cleanliness in mind, developing a precise, clean and thin typeface. Since the "O"

happened to be in the center I placed the publication's official name inside of it.

I did all the cover illustrations except for number three, on which Risa, my eldest daughter who was still in high school, drew the clouds. I airbrushed the sunrays. My favorite is number one, where I showed three stages of a hospital scene, past, present and future, using the appropriate medium and technique for each era.

Number five illustrates a story on a college graduate starting her medical career. I depicted the process by changing her clothes, but people joked that I was good at stripping girls of their costumes.

I also worked on *Supervisor Nurse*. The covers, for political reasons, were usually exterior shots of hospitals, nurses working, etc., which were all supplied. I did some illustrations inside, and the one I like best is the inkblot with a sheep and a lion to portray assaultive behavior of mental patients.

These illustrations show how I use many kinds of art materials and methods, and often combine them in one project. I've used ink, acrylic paint, pastels, dyes, oil-pastels, color overlays, etc. I believe there is no set way to express one's artistic inspirations.

PROJECTS FOR
HOLIDAY SEASONS

Way back when I still had some spare time, I entered many design-related contests with the hope of winning some awards. I mainly entered local contests, such as the Christmas Seals contest sponsored by the Heart Association. I entered three times and won an honorable mention each time. It was easy since good artists probably didn't have any time. But it was still exciting to win because of the awards ceremonies and newspaper coverage.

I designed three greeting cards in the early 70s. The one in the back is a die-cut of one piece of paper that can be folded flat. The Origami crane card was for a New Year's greeting card (perfect for Japan Air Lines). The dove-shaped card actualy flies, carrying a message, "Let's get it off the ground, man!" It was a hope for peace in Vietnam.

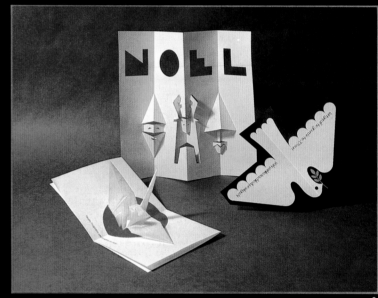

1 Christmas tree ornaments with design based on 12 Days of Christmas were printed on silver foil. Cubes can be assembled without glue. Triangle-shaped tabs at top and bottom lock together automatically.

2 Christmas Seals design for 1970.

3 Three card designs for holiday seasons.

4 Newspaper coverage on awards.

5 Another Christmas Seals design for 1969, using the 12 Days of Christmas theme.

1

NEEDLEWORK ILLUSTRATION

Cross-stitch is one of many embroidery techniques, and as the name implies, each small square in the fabric is covered by colored thread in the shape of a cross. It's all handwork and very time consuming, so it stays within the boundaries of hobby work, not for commercial applications.

If a pattern repeats itself, you don't have to watch very carefully. But if the pattern is complex, almost like a painting, the stitcher has to pay the utmost attention. Even a mistake as little as one cross would eventually set off the format, and you would have to redo the section, according to Yoshiko who did the work.

I made all the designs on graph paper with colored pencils, and she had to follow the pattern one stitch at a time . . . luckily, she didn't play tennis then.

This section is another good example of my philosophy that earlier experiences echo what I design today. I enthusiastically watched cowboy movies and sang country and western music, and you can see that era in works displayed here.

Needlework is a passion of many people throughout the world, but I don't believe many people have tackled a project as large and complex as this series, with the probable exception of tapestry makers of old. We must be either geniuses or fools (probably the latter), since this labor of love seldom generates financial reward.

Most of the needlework displayed here was

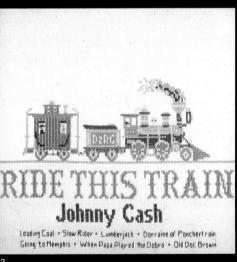

2

3

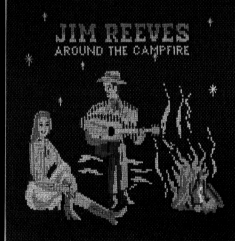

4

1 *New store opening promotion for McDonald's: ''Our family welcomes your family.''*
2 *Record jacket for Johnny Cash's ''Ride this train.''*
3 *Collection of sacred songs by the late great Hank Williams, Sr. entitled, ''I saw the light.''*
4 *''Around the campfire,'' by the late Jim Reeves.*
5 *Marty Robbins' ''Gunfighters' ballads and trail songs.''*
6 *''Riverboat'' by Faron Young. Here, the title was done with regular typography.*

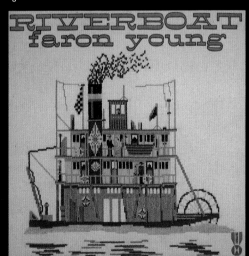

created a long time ago when we were still in Japan. The record jacket designs were submitted to the Nissenbi (Japan Advertising Art) contest and rejected. It is ironic that these same pieces were on a page of Outstanding American Illustrators II, published by Graphic-sha. I guess you almost have to understand the American way of life and love country music to appreciate them.

It was a nightmare when we tackled a 12-piece calendar based on an Old West theme. It took us half a year, with the help of neighbors stitching non-critical parts. We entered the annual craft contest sponsored by Shufu-no-tomo (Housewife's Friend), a leading Japanese magazine for women, and notice of winning second place reached Yoshiko the

day after I left for the U.S. She bought a nice big pearl ring with the award money.

I haven't used this calendar commercially, except for some small sections. I would like to find a sponsor who would use the entire collection. We can change the year and dates easily, and can make some adjustments in the patterns. It would be very unique when printed on linen-textured paper.

Dick Helland wanted to use a needlework for McDonald's new store opening promotion. Resembling "Home Sweet Home" cross-stitch work, we created a piece to be used in a light box and also small tents on tables. I understand they were received favorably.

Judd Gibbons, a young art director from the

same company, saw this piece and wanted to use it for Nestlé chocolates for their newly-developed morsel dolls. Since the borders have smooth lines, we employed a different embroidery method, crewel, in this case. According to Judd, this piece won many design awards.

I am planning to design a revolutionary children's picture book, constructed in a completely different manner. A young reader can select the course of the story as they go through the pages of the book, to build creative and decision-making ability. I will use different styles of illustration, each appropriate for an episode, and needlework would be used for expressing America's South. Stay tuned!

1

2

3

4

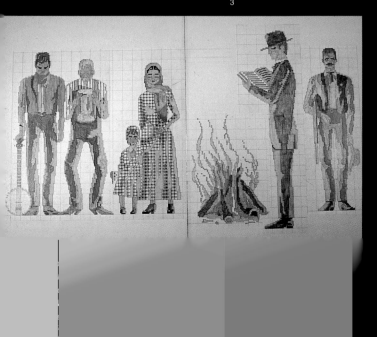

8-19 *Twelve sheets of calendar on the Old West theme. I spent a lot of time researching this. For example, the music sheet in photo 13 is functional, and numbers on the roulette wheel in photo 17 are accurate. It was hard to come up with a proper picture for each month, but I tried . . . the rodeo is held in February, a cold beer for July, a trip on the Mississippi River in August, a cookbook and a turkey for November, and a Christmas prayer scene for December.*

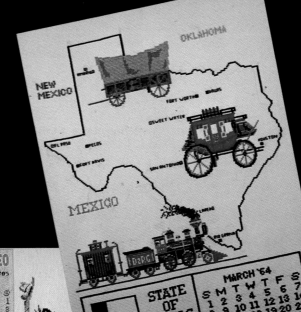

10

8

9

11

12

13

14

15

Most of my new assignments come from referrals, through friends, and above all, satisfied customers. But there is a limit to referral business, especially if you are looking for prospective clients from outside of your area.

I placed ads in *Advertising Age* and *Adweek's Art Director's Index* to market my graphic services. I promoted my logo design and corporate identity capabilities thinking these were the most lucrative ventures. I received inquiries from as far away as Turkey.

The promo piece on the left is a potpourri of my favorite symbols. These designs do not need any explanation other than the names of the organizations to be understood.

The ad to the lower left states that each organization should have a proper image to express their character, products or services. I did this by depicting famous people with different heads. When I put Hitler's head on Marilyn Monroe's body, I knew I would get complaints. But the message I wanted to get across was: Many companies project an improper image through poor corporate identity efforts.

On the right is a promotion using a drinking mug. Since the American idiom, "My cup of tea," means "I'm good at this," or "I excel in this area," I enclosed an accordion-fold pamphlet mentioning all the services I provide, along with tea bags from other parts of the world.

On the far right is a spin-off of the before and after idea. I compared the new logos I designed to the old ones, indicating how bold and modern the new ones were. Of course, I am aware that some people still prefer the old ones.

The "Yech!" ad on the lower right shows delicacies from Japan that would be abhorred in the United States. The message is that you have to understand both nations completely in order to succeed in international communication.

The two symbols on the far lower right show a "before and after" of my own logo. When I left Playboy in 1975, I chose the name "Rising Sun Design," and created a symbol depicting the sun rising in stages. My plan was that as the company grew, I would use the corresponding design. Then I had a few experiences that told me an anti-Japanese feeling still existed in some parts of the country, but more than that, I found out that there was once a whore house in New Orleans called "The House of the Rising Sun."

Anyway, I changed the name to Design 1, which could be interpreted as Number 1. I combined a lower case D and number 1 for the symbol.

68

3

4

Our Cup of Tea

5

6

 design1

8

1 Collection of my favorite symbols for a page in Art Director's Index.

2 "Misfits!" promo piece switching heads and bodies of famous people.

3-5 "Our cup of tea" promotion. Pamphlet, along with tea bags in a mug, were hand-delivered to clients and friends.

6 "Before and after" ad in Ad Age contrasts newly-designed logos next to old ones.

7 "Yech!" ad depicts differences of tastes of two nations.

8 Our own "before and after" logos. Progressive symbol for Rising Sun Design and symbol and logotype for Design 1.

ESF Design and Desktop Publishing Course

02077

Inside Design

Goldsholl

DEDICATION

I dedicate this,

my first book, to

Millie Goldsholl

who has shared my life

and work

as well as the

joys and tears

incurred

in the search for

meaning.

The photograph on the first page
is from one of my favorite design projects.
This was an annual report for
Kimberly Clark Corporation and was
one of 11 reports I designed for the company.

My design work for annual reports has often
included discussions with the company
on theme and subject.
Although the writing is the responsibility of
others I have been privileged to participate
in determining what the company
said about itself as well as designing the book.

In this case, the theme of the KC report of 1969
was suggested to and accepted by the
Secretary of the Company, Mr. Roger Baird,
a particularly astute client.
It was decided that the book would become
a world report on the company
and the illustrations were to be on
their best known product "Kleenex Tissues".*
The use of their crepe tissue was world wide
and we gathered packaging from each country
to photograph for the inside pages.

An appropriate graphic theme was designed
for each country and a roll of the specific
material was used as a prop.

The Japanese version was the most striking
and became the cover of the report.
Other examples of the interior graphics are
shown inside this book.

INSIDE DESIGN
A REVIEW: 40 YEARS OF WORK

GOLDSHOLL

CONTENTS

ISBN 4-7661-0417-X
Printed in Japan
First edition April 1987
Graphic-sha Publishing Co., Ltd.
1-9-12, Kudan-Kita, Chiyoda-ku
Tokyo 102, Japan
Telephone (03) 263-4318
Facsimile (03) 263-5297
Telex J29877 GRAPHIC

ACKNOWLEDGMENTS

There were many who inspired me, to grow and mature enough to give meaning to my life as a designer and film maker.
There were those who worked with me. There were those I worked for as well as many who were my teachers and friends. And there were a precious few who are etched more deeply into my past.

My father gave me life and ethics, taught me the meaning of integrity and the value of living a simple life, a facet so easily forgotten in the pressure of business, competition and ego.

My teacher, Lazslo Moholy-Nagy inspired me to combine my first love, to paint and draw, and my work as a commercial artist into a new world of design, awareness and concern for human values and to a broader vision.

More recently, Dr. Jacob Bronowski, mathematician, scientist and poet, showed me how it was possible to reach millions of people at once and share with them a deep knowledge of nature and science as well as an appreciation of great art. Like Moholy, he reached people. His gift to us, the epic series "The Ascent of Man" remains the classic of its genre. His concern for design was evident in his speech to an Aspen Design Conference on "Design and Human Values". It was another turning point in my life. He said that "it was easier to create the illusion of fulfillment rather than offer people real fulfillment . . . the designer has to choose between a drug or a food."

My dear friend, Dr. Robert Leslie, gave me my first one person show at his A-D Gallery in New York in 1950. He was, more than anyone, able to lift my sense of worth about my own work.

Egbert Jacobson, Director of Design for Container Corporation of America gave me my first design projects of higher challenge. He was an elegant task master and an inspiration. I worked on company projects and also worked on his books, on "Trademark Design" and "Basic Color".

William Stuart, President of Martin Senour Paints was a client for 15 years. Spencer Stuart, who was a Director of Design for the company has remained a lifelong client and friend. I still share in his work no matter where his business interests go.

Tom Ware, President of International Minerals & Chemicals, was an imaginative and vigorous partner in our search together for a true image for that fine company.

Ham Grigg, CEO at Seven-Up, a provoking client, challenged me constantly and evoked constant new ideas in our work together. I had the difficult assignment to redesign *his* design for the Seven-Up trademark.

Roger Baird, Secretary of Kimberly Clark Corporation and I shared ten years of annual report designs. Together we took the company to a most interesting new level of design and a more effective use of their printing paper.

And Hy Hoffman, Brand Manager at Kimberly Clark, helped me to introduce a fresh look in the design of the company graphics and packaging. He was the first to ask us to make a film for industry. "Texoprint" was very successful and drove Millie Goldsholl and me into full film production.

Ed Russell, Vice President and Marketing Director at Champion Papers, gave me my first documentary film assignment. He was a superb and astute client, demanding and receiving a fine production.

Gene Senya, Marketing Director at Eastman Kodak gave us two films for the company, both on the essence of photography.

I must also include my friends Jane and Bernie Sahlins, the leading figures of the 1986 International Theatre Festival of Chicago. For them I designed the major symbolism for the event and from them I also got a new sense of the living theatre.

Finally, I must credit my associates, more than employees, some as long as thirty-three years. I enjoyed working with John Weber, designer, Master Calligrapher, by my side. We spent endless hours searching for the "best" design. He is still working with me. Tom Miller began with me simultaneously and he too spent all these years as a designer and production artist, with multiple skills and enormous patience. Nor can I forget Jim Logan, graduate design engineer from the School of Design. Together we invented new things, products, models, machines and eventually our first computer for the animation camera which he programmed as well.

Like the frames in a film, the names of others come to mind, some passed quickly, others still remain. All helped to evolve the spirit and essence of Goldsholl Associates. Each brought some special skill and the sum was a broader design capability.

Among them: in design Mel Linn, my first assistant, David Foster, Kate Bertell, Fred Nomiya, Zeke Ziner, Jim Lunde, Fred Ota, Victor Ing, John Siena, Bob Hunter, Bonnie Bluestein, Susan Keig, Jay Williams, Ed Bedno, Renee & Don Walkoe, Jim Neill, and currently, Brigit Rameika.

And in film: Wayne Boyer and Larry Janiak, the first film assistants, Paul Jessel, currently Animation Director, Nick Kolias, Production Manager and Editor, Pete Dakis, Dan Chessher, Marie Cenkner, Ken Mundie and Kelley Ray.

Our present company, Goldsholl Design & Film, includes two associates in work and management. This has become a unique consortium of designers and film makers. Along with Millie Goldsholl, Executive Film Producer, my son, Harry Goldsholl, is president of the Film Group. He is a cinematographer and a computer graphics specialist. He and the others have brought new growth and direction to what once began as a small free lance office. We are emerging into new areas of activity in keeping with the current need.

This book represents my personal work done with a few assistants. All examples are my own except in such cases where I strongly influenced the results. Where work was done in common, the names of my associates will be credited in the captions. The work shown was done between the years 1945 and 1985.

I also acknowledge my debt to Yoshi Sekiguchi who urged me to undertake this fairly difficult task, to find and notate my findings from disorganized slide archives. It has become a nostalgic trip. He and his lovely wife, Yoshiko, found the publisher, arranged the details, fed all of us sushi in countless meetings and, with his pretty daughter, Chika, did all the keylining and production. Ray Andrews edited my handwritten text, also placing commas and colons in proper places.

Finally, I acknowledge my life with my wife, Millie, with whom I have shared 47 years of work and love. Our work together, mostly in film, has been revealing, tumultous and satisfying. She has helped me to see more clearly, to remain objective and retain my sense of values.

Without all the above this book would be far less.

Thank you all,

Morton Goldsholl
July, 1986

4

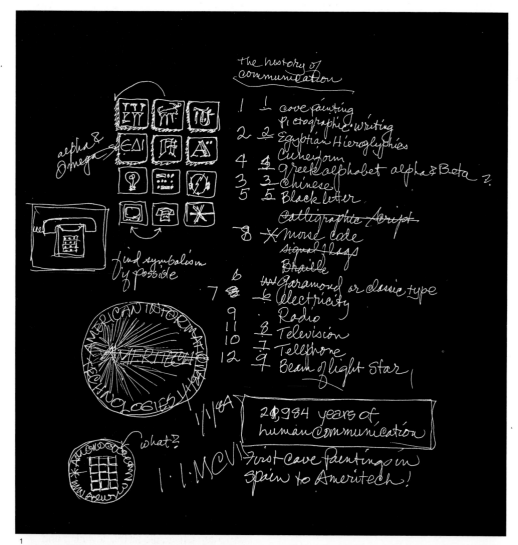

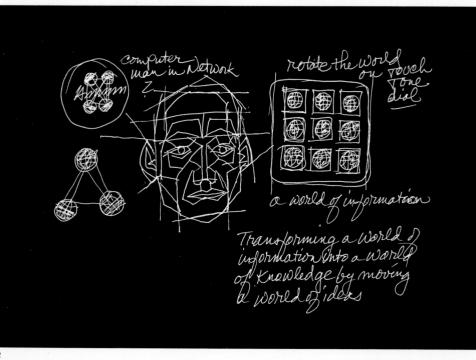

INTRODUCTION

This book is not intended to become more
than it is. It is simply a retrospective collection
of my work in design and film,
a segment of 40 years in my life.
It began with my first contact with a new
philosophy at the School of Design
in Chicago, American Bauhaus it was called,
brought here by Walter Paepcke, President of
Container Corporation of America who
undoubtedly was influenced by his Director
of Design, Egbert Jacobson.

It was Moholy-Nagy's school, an exciting place,
filled with great teachers, Gyorgy Kepes
among them. There were visiting lecturers,
Walter Gropius, Leger, Bunuel, and many
artists and film makers.

The new design I encountered demanded
a sense of awareness that previous work and
experience never evoked.

It was the act of becoming aware that
changed my life. It meant to recognize the
tactile quality of paper as well as the printability.
It meant that design was more than
two dimensional graphics, that it was
architecture, the design of tools and furniture
and objects for use.
It also meant that designers could change the
world along with the engineers and scientists
who also were engaged in the effort.
Among the deeper lessons, we learned that
good design was a fulfillment and bad design
was useless and a sham.

It was evident that design must go beyond
helping a corporate client to just
sell things but also to reach the ultimate client,
the consumer, with a useful and
handsome solution.

This has been the stated and driving principle
of my work as a designer and film maker
and one of the reasons for this book.
My hope is that it will fulfill
for many more students the message
I delivered in hundreds of talks over the years
to art schools and designer groups.

1 *An Ameritech project required research on the major
leaps in communications over the ages. The telephone
touch dial was vehicle for the various visual symbols.*

2 *Many new sketches preceded designs and symbolism
describing the new digital network the company
is building.*

5

INSIDE DESIGN

There are many opinions about what design is and what design is not. Almost as many as there are designers.

That is one interesting aspect about design that is often overlooked. The diversity establishes that there can be almost as much freedom in this work as there is in free art, in painting, in drawing or sculpture.

A designer accepts a new responsibility once the decision is made to work for others. But I cannot believe my life in design has been restricted.

I can choose my work and can accept or reject a design project. Hundreds of approaches to answering a design problem are open to me. Often, I can suggest changes in a product or process which will enhance it, increase its value, make it more useful or even look better. This is not restriction.

The disciplines of design occur only in the choices. We can choose a client, product or a whole system of information to help, if it is useful to do so. We can choose the elements and ingredients of design to make the sketch, the package or the illustration.

There are millions of choices and decisions in each phase of the work. They are delicate decisions made in micro seconds as to the color, size of type or other elements to be used. This is the life of a working designer. But in no way can this be considered inhibiting or restrictive.

Being able to say no as well as yes gives the designer as much freedom as the artist.

There was more conformity in the past. There were written rules and guidelines. Layouts were thus and so, type and art were subject less to fancy and more to rote. As trends evolved and one designer followed another into the golden spotlight of success and acclaim, we also heard "to design is to plan".

We were handed hard, fast rules of typography, told to letterspace caps, indent the first line of a paragraph, always begin a segment of information with a large cap, lead lines widely, never run flush left ragged right, align into strict columns never more than 55 characters long, and so on, endlessly.

I remember once, in those early days of my career, arguing in a public forum on typography with a great designer of the time who insisted that what the world of design needed was a manual of typographic practice. It was evident in his own work he would never follow this manual.

The next generation of designers brought about an enormous change in this aspect of design.

Caps were tightly packed even overlapping. Paragraphs were not indented but given extra line spacing.

Lines, packed flush left, ragged right, almost has become standard and a lazy way to set type. It was just as uncaring as the original flush left and right style it replaced since the lines were never broken for *sense*.

Meaning must be the measure of design. When the designers of the Bauhaus "threw lines of type at the page" they seemed to always land so that important things were readable.

What seemed random and casual freed the uses of typography up. Fonts were mixed and manipulated. But the angular, constructivist or stacatto effect was directed toward the meaning of the words, emphasizing the important subject.

THE EFFECT OF DESIGN

Awareness as to the effect of his work is the first major goal of the emerging designer.

Technical skills such as drawing, photography, film making, illustration, graphic production, art, spacing type, lettering, knowledge of printing and of paper unfortunately are just the beginning.

The fulfillment of a design does not end with the delivery of final art for production. In fact, that is where it begins.

Contained in that keyline or film is the means to affect people, seduce or inform them, change their lives, feed them real food, give them health, awareness and satisfaction.

That's what the design of a package, book, product, car, house, advertisement, commercial or film can do.

Moholy once said that designers can lead the world. I smile at the thought but agree that designers might change the world since they are important participants in the means of production and very close to the leaders of the process.

This is why it is a designer's responsibility to remain objective, even under the heavy pressure of client prejudice. To best serve both client and consumers, he must remain the bridge between the clients and their consumers devoting all energies to serving both equally well.

Without sales there cannot be usefulness. Without usefulness there will be no sales. Without either there would be no need for design in this country and in our time.

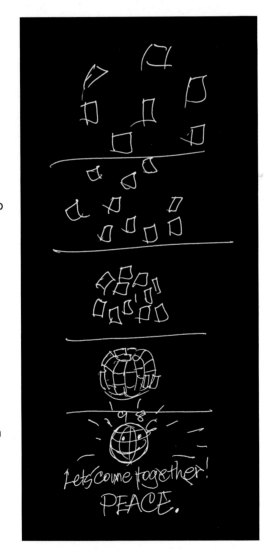

We try to create a greeting card each year. Each one becomes a hope for lasting peace.

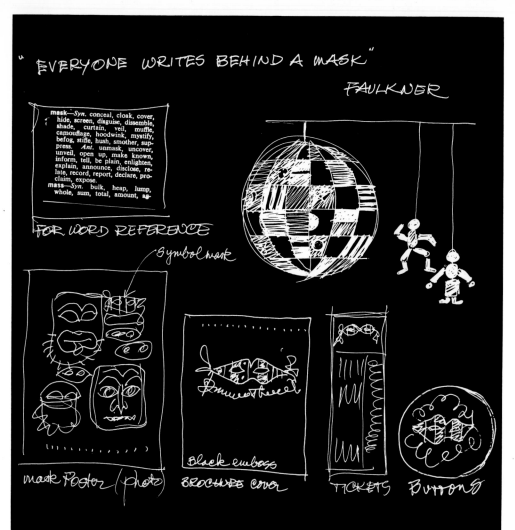

"*EVERYONE WRITES BEHIND A MASK*"

FAULKNER

mask—*Syn.* conceal, cloak, cover, hide, screen, disguise, dissemble, shade, curtain, veil, muffle, camouflage, hoodwink, mystify, befog, stifle, hush, smother, suppress. *Ant.* unmask, uncover, unveil, open up, make known, inform, tell, be plain, enlighten, explain, announce, disclose, relate, record, report, declare, proclaim, expose.
mass—*Syn.* bulk, heap, lump, whole, sum, total, amount, ag-

FOR WORD REFERENCE

Symbol mask

mask Poster (photo)   *BROCHURE cover*   *Black emboss*   *TICKETS*   *BUTTONS*

1

1 *The Chicago International Theatre Festival of 1986 filled my sketchbook for months. There were so many possibilities. The history of the theatre is enormous.*
2 *The hand puppet can become a world symbol too.*

7

HOW I WORK

My work in design has few rules.
I have no set agenda. The only sense of direction is to understand the need. I listen, listen, ask a few questions and listen again.

  "Listen with your ears, eyes and mind."

That lesson I learned long ago. People speak in many ways. They reveal their strengths and fears, insecurities and concerns in how they see things and describe their feelings about a project.

When I have thought about the project for some time, anywhere from 1 day to a week, I will begin to sketch ideas, write thoughts and try to reach into the design.
I continue to reach and even overreach.
If an idea is good, it still may not be the best.
The best is never achieved until I reach to failure.

Constant trial and error is the only way to find new things, create new images or new film design.

Although the above seems indecisive it is really not. It's simply the way I solve my problems. Fluidity and free exploration is the key to the answers I'm seeking. It is so in design and in my relationships with clients and associates who work with me.

Analysing your idea in your mind is the easiest way to design before you sketch.
And sketch I do. My notebooks are filled with scribbles, thumbnail sketches, and many words related to the subject. Design to me is also finding ideas in words. I will often write slogans, copy headlines, and find exciting quotes to stimulate that simplest, purest visual symbol into my mind.

I will show my clients any amount of the work they wish to see. But I always have strong reasons why my choice should be accepted.

This process has seldom failed. I listened, learned, thought, sketched and developed the design.

And like most designers there are times when I have a creative block. Nothing happens. And I have no formula to change this.

In the beginning of my career, every detail of the design and execution was mine to resolve. I believe any concerned designer feels that responsibility, heavily. There can be no personal escape if any detail is flawed. This haunts all of us.

Later though, my work changed. As a result of Moholy's influence, I was intrigued by new projects that were beyond print. Others joined my studio and the simple, difficult life of a free lance designer was no longer for me.

Very capable people who shared my view joined me as my work grew in dimensional design, in packaging, products, furniture design and interiors using a rich variety of materials and technologies. My interest in special experimental photography, light experiments and motion picture films was also growing as a result of the School of Design. Films became an obsession since I found that people responded to our films far more strongly than to any print design.

Millie Goldsholl, who studied full time at the school and had majored in Architecture, also joined me in the studio as a film maker, designer, director, producer and editor.
It was chaotic and a constant turmoil to be involved in so many things. But the associates who joined us had special skills.
I could now overcome my lack of knowledge in the new media and disciplines since I learned what they knew.

2

INSPIRATION AND EMOTION

The emotional aspect of design is the same in any act of creating a work of art. A design, any design, cannot become finalized without some passion, (a devotion to the spirit of the work) a deep feeling about the nature of what needs to be done.

No new form, image, visual, graphic or sculptural statement can ever evolve from a designer's mind without going to the wellspring of human thought and feeling. No new form can ever appear unless there is an inspired moment, a spark of extra feeling and a resulting joy of the discovery.

Every artist I know, working in art, music, literature, in the crafts or theater, has felt that rush of feeling and will agree that there are moments of such concentrated energy when everything seems to go right.

No one can be a genius all the time. Genius, as seen in Einstein, DaVinci and the others, included a unique capability to see the present and the future at once and the effect their discoveries might have on mankind.

Designers must have a small increment of that genius capability to be able to create a truly useful design. The design of a trademark can affect a corporation enormously, influencing it and the fortunes of its people for years to come.

The design of a corporate system of graphics can create or destroy a favorable aura around any company, including the projection of the ethic by which the organization lives and works.

Walter Paepcke, head of Container Corporation, was a great business leader who understood the value of such design. He and Egbert Jacobson gave the company a superb design program by inviting leading designers and artists to fulfill all the needs of the corporation.

He was a passionate man, totally devoted to these principles and he built these strong beliefs into his entire company. His leadership and insight gave the company a top position in the packaging industry. Human imagination derives from this passion, from intuition and feeling, from the inner senses and an instantaneous response to what is right or wrong.

There is a time to choose by intuition rather than by statistical research. I believe I share this feeling with many of my most respected and successful colleagues.

WHY DESIGN?

I have chosen design and film as my life's work. I have not given up other activity in doing so. There have been rewards beyond belief including the joys of knowing my colleagues in this field, and the recognitions that were given to me on all too many occasions. There have been almost a thousand lectures and talks in my life, time with young students and peers in design. I have met great men who have deep values and concerns for the work we do and the society we work in. I have discovered new things, images and processes.

Among the normal joys there have been concerns, doubts and some anxieties. Commercial work has brought me face to face with the deeper issues of our society. Inescapable questions about advertising that demeans people, portraying women and men as distortions, prattling on about soap detergent or grease spots, promising more, seducing more and fulfilling less.

I have had great clients. There was a mutual respect and an interdependence. I felt I was a partner with the company, devoted to the whole task, creating an aura that reflected the integrity and meaning of the organization. Concern for design and designers is an act of awareness in a company.

1 Childview was interesting because it dealt with symbolism for film, learning and fantasy for children.
2 Children have a special glow and inspired a pageful of sketches.

8

Paint manufacturers have given me many assignments. I designed for Martin Senour Paints, Sears, Montgomery Ward and Illinois Bronze at different times. These were exploratory sketches seeking a name and theme for a corporation and a brand logotype.

Design for the corporation offers great opportunities for a designer. Often there is a design of the company logotype and/or symbol, the identification system, signage and stationery.
There is always the annual report and facilities brochures and packaging. There is much to do.

Winning such assignments is the objective of most graphics designers and rightfully so.
There is a continuity of work, an acceptance of the designer at all levels of the company.
Once accepted, the designer can influence management decisions in regard to image, products, interiors, advertising and help to build what is now called a corporate culture.

This is not an easy arena to enter.
A designer must devote time to his client.
Not just board time, but learning and listening time. It is necessary to reach a point in time, perhaps a matter of months or years, when the designer really knows the company.
A time when he understands its products, services, goals, sense of integrity, people, competitors and marketplace at least as well as the management.
Even then the designer must remain an objective observer and not swayed by personalities or executive prejudices.

A design program need not begin or end with a trademark. Yet it still is often the most effective vehicle the company has to present the corporate face. In some cases the company image, truly and imaginatively projected, can even modify the corporation standing in the financial world.

The designer can remain with a company for many years if the above is understood, practiced and fully appreciated.

Finally, it is absolutely necessary for a designer to believe in the company, its stated objectives and its products.

I have been honored with more than my share of fine clients, some of whose design programs appear here. If longevity is a measure, they have worked with me for many years, the least 8 years, the longest 15.

9

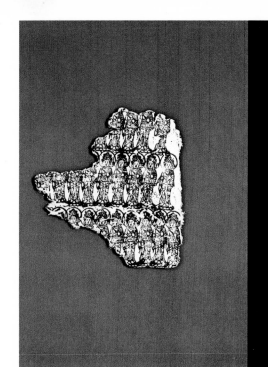

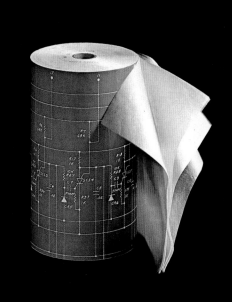

Kimberly Clark: Annual Report for 1969

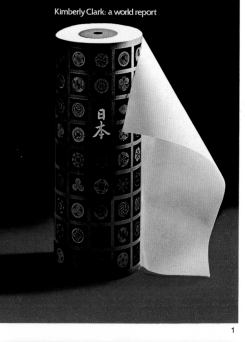
Kimberly Clark: a world report

1

visited nearly a dozen Kimberly-Clark installations including the big plant at Beech Island and the engineering center at Neenah, Wisconsin.

The trips make sense because at Kimberly-Clark production equipment and technology enjoy an unusual universality. Machinery can be interchanged from plant to plant with only slight modifications to make products suitable for the local market.

For this reason, technical people can also be easily exchanged. One U.S. engineer claims he can walk into a Kimberly-Clark plant anywhere in the world and tell quickly if things are going well by the sound of the machines. Mares puts it this way:

"All types of problems crop up in a new operation like Prudhoe. We can eliminate one of the unknowns by putting in a tissue machine we understand and converting equipment that has already proved itself. We're putting the best Kimberly-Clark ideas into Prudhoe and it should turn out to be the company's best mill, wouldn't you say?"

Maybe. But technicians of the Peter J. Schweitzer Group look at this question somewhat differently. They practice the "finest art" of papermaking, producing super-thin papers and technical grades that are turned out slowly by tissue making standards but superbly by the standards of customers worldwide.

They are building a new plant at Barbosa, Colombia, which is expected to begin operation this summer. Flax grown in Colombia, and possibly other locally grown fibers, will be used for pulp.

Exact attention to production detail is critical, so every element of personnel training and plant operation is supervised by a corps of Schweitzer experts. Among them: Joe Master, head of research and development at the company's plant in Spotswood, New Jersey, and a craftsman with nearly 30 years' experience.

"We used to export our papers to Colombia. Now we're going to manufacture there, a good arrangement in many respects. But our customers will

The paper towel is revolutionizing kitchen routines for the German housewife. Kimberly-Clark's subsidiary, Zellwolle, has set the quality standard with its Kleenex brand, preferred by a majority of consumers. Another popular product, our heavy-duty disposable handkerchief, almost doubled its sales in 1968.

2   3

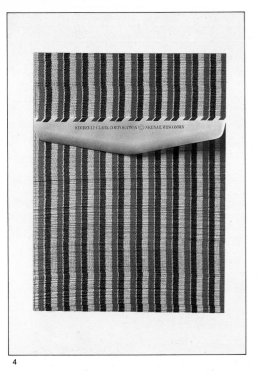

4

5

6

A WORLD REPORT

There is a special responsibility to the design of a corporate financial report.
Once a year this brochure must reach the shareholder with the status of the company, the value of the stock, the dramatic events of the year and the sense of future developments.

The report of 1969 was intended to show how universal Kimberly Clark tissue products were worldwide, how consistent the quality was and yet how well they answered the diverse needs and desires of each region.

The report of 1968 faced still another challenge. Kimberly Clark needed to demonstrate to graphic designers that their papers were richly varied in color, texture and content.
This report was designed to intrigue the imagination of the designers and paper specifiers.

The book was printed on five different papers. Two were laminated to produce the cover which was then die cut into a portfolio to hold a collection of single pages and two bound inserts. One insert was the financial report and the second a full color brochure on a newly developed non-woven fabric.

1 *The covers of the 1969 report printed in A-Z form. The financials were stapled into one leg of the Z and the editorial into the other.*
2 *The inside spread on Germany showing how the products of each country were shown.*
3 *Thailand, 1969 report*
4 *Back cover of 1966 report*
5 *Back cover of new product booklet*
6 *Single page insert 1968 report*
7 *Cover of 1968 report*
8 *France, 1969 report*
9 *Australia, 1969 report*
10 *Holland, 1969 report*

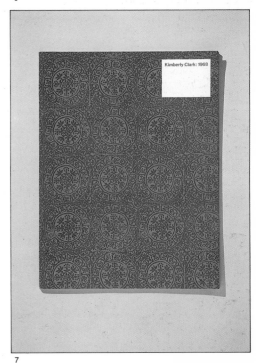

11

7

8

9

10

CONSUMER PACKAGING

In 1960 I participated in an exciting and memorable design project with Kimberly Clark Corporation. It was a major design study to examine and develop a series of new packages for Kleenex Tissues.
The effort was broadly based, to explore freely, develop new graphics, containers and opening devices.
In a sense, new appeals were to be found to reach for segments of the market that were not fully tapped.

Kimberly Clark is market driven, as a great company must be. It has always analyzed its appeal in the marketplace and the research studies it conducts have measured the visual impact and viability of its consumer products.
It remains one of the most design sensitive corporations since its products are among the best known in the world.

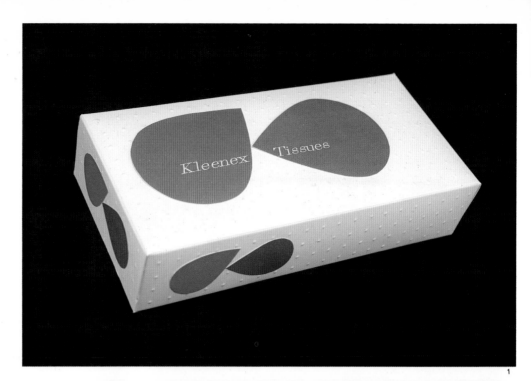

1

2

3

4

12

One of the unique experiments was to surround the package with competitors and photograph them all in and out of focus to test how effective the design would be.

The shapes of the packages and the uniqueness of the experimental constructions were much more diverse.

There were "purse-packs", rounded to the hand rather than rectangular.
There were air-foil types, three of which were connected by spot gluing to hold 600 tissues.
There were special opening devices to lift and dispense without tearing anything.
Triangular packs were bound together by a sleeve and the most unique experiment was to deboss a series of dots out of the material so that the slight tactile roughness in the hand could emphasize the smoothness of the tissue.
This project remains one of the most extensive exploratory package design studies I have ever done.

5

Not all these designs were practical
and the company chose wisely to research
these devices before use. Some were adopted.

In all, the experiment was a demonstration of
how free design exploration could bring
so many new ideas and potentially
useful suggestions to these products
and to the marketplace.
This is true with most products and
packages in many corporations.
Fear of disturbing an important product has
often stifled needed improvements.
Change for change's sake is poor planning.
Resisting necessary change is even poorer.

Kimberly Clark has always moved toward
change and the design experiences I had with
the company were positive and fruitful.

My associate, John Weber, was closely
associated with this development.

1 *The experimental package with debossed surface*
2 *Mass photo setup*
3 *Visibility and recognition study*

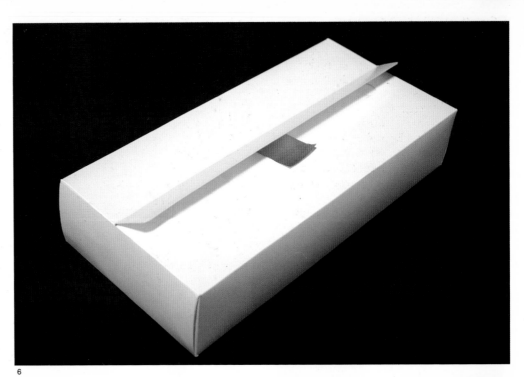
6

8

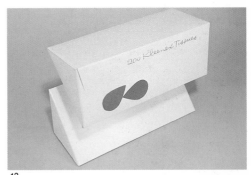
7

13

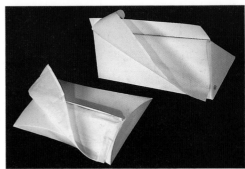
9

10

11

12

13

14

4 *Out-of-focus test for legibility of the symbol*
5 *Purse type package, the favorite in all the tests*
6 *Trial opening strip*
7 *Trial packages*
8 *Design for shipping containers with new symbol in 1 color.*
9 *Triangular packs*
10 *Color tests and opening tests*
11 *Air foil forms*
12 *Triangular packs*
13 *Air foil forms*
14 *Purse packs*

GRAPHICS AND PACKAGING

There were many other packages
and graphic pieces designed during this period.
One special package for Bond paper
featured a large feather quill pen and series of
circles all printed in gold. This package is
now 24 years old and has not changed.
Other graphic experiments on Kleenex Tissues
were tried. None were successful although
one package made use of hot stamped foil
circles which were striated at various
angles allowing the package to flicker
as one walked by.

There were also many brochures and
advertisements created for other
divisions of the company.

1 *Quill feather box for Kimberly Clark Business papers*
2 *Hot stamp and embossed package*
3 *Information sheet on Texoprint*
4 *Cover for the 1971 report*
5 *Package Graphics trial*
6 *Package Graphics trial*
7 *Advertisement for Erasable Bond*

14

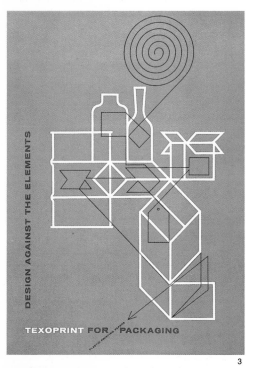

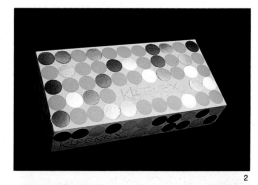

The most meaningful contribution the designer can make to a corporate client is to become totally involved in the company work and life. Certainly, the design staff of the company seems to do exactly that, and the director of the department could probably fulfill the need for developing and managing, often designing the whole design program, including the trademark.

However, there are many strings attached to the inside designer who is subject to the pressures and prejudices of management and unable to express a point of view that might endanger the employee in such a position.

The consultant often is brought in by the director for two reasons. First, the experience and design record of the consultant may span work done for dozens of companies on similar projects.
Secondly, the designer brought in remains objective, resists pressure and can say no without fear of losing a job, but only one assignment.

The Design system must begin with the trademark, the logotype and/or symbol. It can be wholly original, or an update or modification of the original. In any case the system must include a manual of practice that guides the use of the mark in all circumstances.

The project may be relatively short, completed in a few months, or very extensive, lasting years.
The longer period may be needed to finally reach into all subsidiaries or the design of the product, interiors, advertising, annual reports, architecture, even corporate exhibits, multi-media shows and motion pictures.

There is much value in the long association a design group can develop with a corporation and remain relatively free.
It certainly is good business to build these relationships for the designer. But the price for this continuity of work is high.
Total commitment to the company will generally be rewarded by 10 to 15 years of fine design projects.

15

The Trademark, once designed, needs total fulfillment. And the application of the design to all the properties and products of a company determines how deeply it will penetrate into the company work. And, it must begin while the original design for the symbol begins.

MARTIN SENOUR PAINTS

This client was the most important of my early career. The company, already foremost in its field, had over 1,000 custom colors and a strong desire to become the most recognized color source in paint by Architects and Interior Designers. My task was to create the new image, apply design to the paint cans, develop devices for the store, the sales force, for displays and advertising.

The first assignment was to revise the color cards. We created a new card strip, more flexible so as to place one color near the next or place the color against furniture or fabrics.

Thousands of new applications followed the design of basic marks for House Paint and Automotive. The design program remained in effect in my office for 15 years, the longest of any of our associations.

The most remarkable achievement of all was our invention of an electronic color mixing machine which obsoleted the hand weighing method and shortened the mixing time from overnight to 60 seconds.
Consumers simply waited for their paint.
The machine could mix, to absolute color match, over two million colors by punch card insertion.
It was truly the "Colorbot" we called it, and it became the standard process of the paint industry. This machine was co-invented with Jim Logan, my associate.
We increased the company sales volume by 50% the first month the machine was introduced.

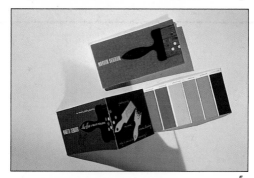

Since the machine was low cost, a truckload of paint was sold with each one.

My client was Bill Stuart, President of the Company, who asked me to take on this extended retainership. Spencer R. Stuart, who was the Director of Advertising and Design was the second reason for my success.

The program brought all of us many awards and recognitions. In this backward, tradition ridden field, this design program was exemplary and prompted many changes in the industry.
Most other alert paint companies then began to examine their packaging and graphics.

1 *Trademark for Automotive Paints – 1951*
2 *The automotive line*
3 *Convention booth detail*
4 *Paint warning card detail*
5 *Color cards*
6 *Color cards in use*
7 *Color chip display*
8 *Color card detail*
9 *Promotional book and collateral*

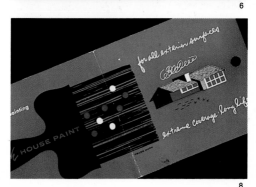

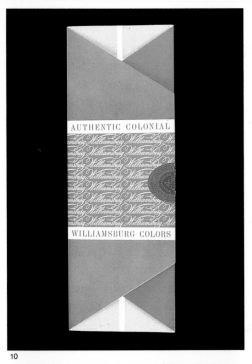

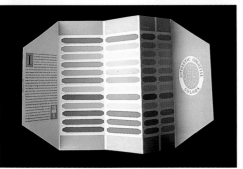

10

11

12

13

17

10 *Folder for Williamsburg Restoration colors*
  Designed with Ed Bedno
11 *Color selection for architects*
12 *Folder for Williamsburg Restoration colors*
13 *Brush Trademark – 1951*
14 *Color display*
15 *Color display*
16 *Corporate Stationery*

14

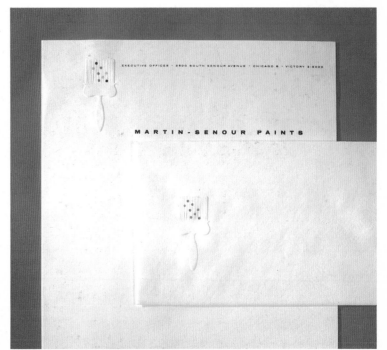

15

16

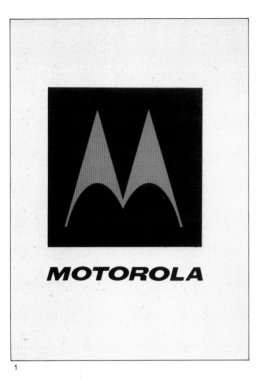

1

2

MOTOROLA

The design program for Motorola was all inclusive. Designing the well-known Motorola M was the beginning. Based on two sine wave forms, the mark was first applied to shipping containers and then to all the forms in print and on products.

This identification system was designed in 1963 and has not changed. The company has grown into a major electronics and transmission equipment firm, but the mark, which had a major impact when introduced, has remained the same with minor modifications.

One of the most interesting projects in the total effort was the assignment to redesign the showroom in the Chicago Merchandise Mart. The work which needed to be completed in a very short time evolved into a major effort.

The showroom was awarded the title of "Showroom of the Year" by Interiors Magazine.

The objective was to give Motorola a whole new image, taking it beyond the automobile radio industry and into what was then the bright new world of television, home entertainment, and radios for people. The styling was reflective of this effort.

The Director of Design was Herb Zeller, a fine product designer, who was responsible for guiding the program into acceptance.

1 *The Motorola Trademark – 1963*
2 *Package Design*
3 *Packaging Program*
4 *Motorola Showroom*
5 *Old and New*
6 *A view of the Showroom from the corridor*
7 *Interior of the Showroom*

18

3

4

5

1

2

FAIRMONT FOODS

Design for a large food company is important in many ways. Food is one of our elemental needs. Serving the food industry has been one of the largest areas of design work for me. There have been dozens of major projects, some in packaging, others that were whole design programs that include the corporate trademark, package design, graphics and annual reports, signage and vehicular identification.

Fairmont Foods in Omaha, Nebraska was one of the latter. Our project included a broad look at the company and its vast product list. There were snack foods, soft drinks and dairy foods. The total design program was fulfilled with annual reports and other collateral print materials.

The effective design began with a ribbon form that was placed on all packages and in all visual media. Colorful applications gave a full sense of variety to this company of hundreds of products. Ice cream and milk were delineated strongly with the basic forms.

This approach, the use of a strong symbolism which was applied to all of the products and print graphics of my clients, has been a keystone of my work in design.

Identification can never be created by a lick and a promise. Consistent application of the mark in a variety of ways is my answer to implanting a company symbol on the mass mind.

In this case, the thousands of products Fairmont marketed in grocery stores across the U.S. helped to fulfill the impression that this company was colorful, had many appetizing products in many categories and each had its own "ribbon award."

20

3

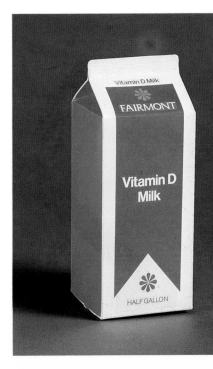

4

5

1 *Ribbon trademark – 1970*
2 *Mass display, milk cartons*
3 *Page from the report*
4 *Milk carton*
5 *Cover photo of annual report*
6 *Cover of annual report with introduction of the symbol – 1971*
7 *Cover of annual report*
8-9 *Proposed package design*

6

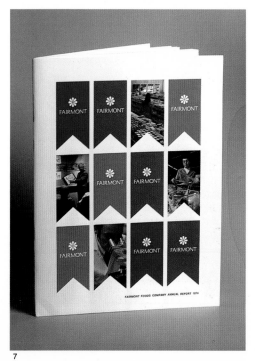

7

8

9

IMC, ADVENTURE IN CHANGE

International Minerals and Chemicals, a client
that remained with me for 10 years,
first came to us with a unique problem.
This fine company, had been paying dividends
to its shareholders for all of 50 years.
It decided to celebrate the anniversary
by embarking on a period of self examination,
to express what IMC really was
along with deciding
how to project this great company to the world
and to the special category of consumers,
the farmers here and abroad.

Symbols were designed to project this
company in a fresh, new way. It produces
minerals for fertilizers for agriculture as one
of its many major products. The design of the
mark was based on one of these minerals.
The phosphate crystal is hexagonal
in the center and pointed at each end.
Cutting across the crystal reveals two
hexagonal faces side by side. In one face,
IMC is placed. In the second a symbolic
''tree of life'', to demonstrate the power of the
mineral to grow plants.
The word ''GROW'' was also
pre-empted, to demonstrate the company
philosophy and to challenge its personnel.

1 *Corporate Symbol – 1959*
2 *Annual Report Cover, 1960*
3 *Modular sign, flexible structure,*
  from 2 to 6 panels
4 *Matchbook gift package*
5 *Fortune ad*
6 *Fortune ad*

22

INTERNATIONAL MINERALS & CHEMICAL CORPORATION 1960 ANNUAL REPORT

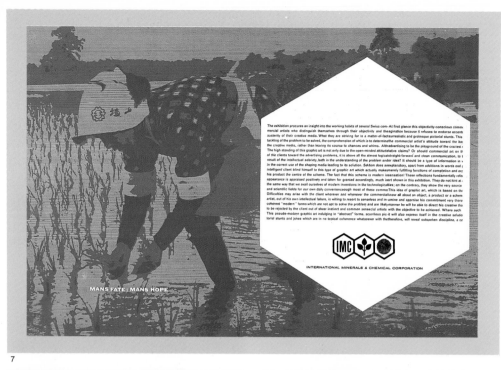

7

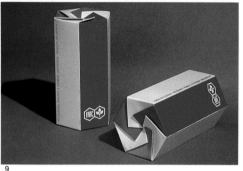

9

10

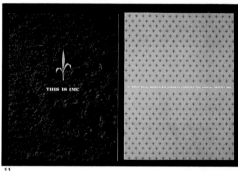

11

7 *Fortune ad*
8 *Gift box of Accent*
9 *Gift box of Accent*
10 *Entrance to Corporate Headquarters*
11 *Brochure*
12 *Fortune ad*
13 *Annual report*
14 *Flag*
15 *Major Highway Sign*

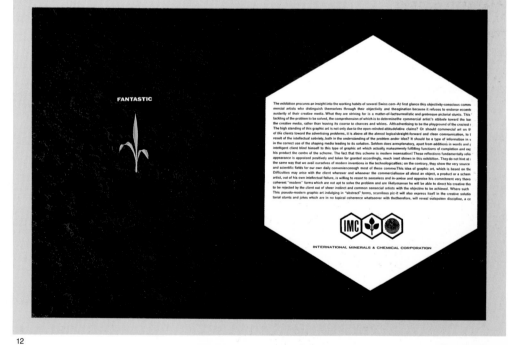

12

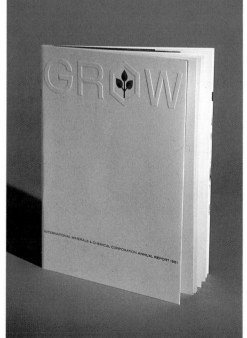

13

14

15

BAXTER TRAVENOL *

This company, a major supplier of IV solutions, pharmaceuticals and medical supplies, was a client for 8 years. In that time we redesigned the corporate image system, designed packaging, signage and created graphics for the annual reports.

The original symbol was redesigned to give greater visual dimension to the form to more clearly portray the depth and importance of the corporate services and philosophy.

My first effort was in the symbol itself and the designs created are shown here. Annual reports which had less distinct visual qualities were brought to a new level of precise and exact imagery. Products were often incorporated in a unique way and a major emphasis on the company personnel was also developed. New technologies and research were emphasized.

24

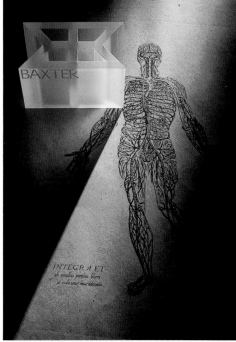

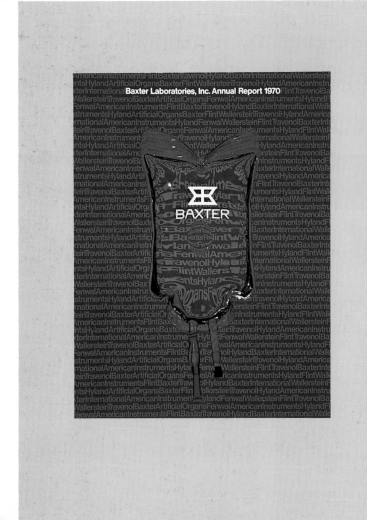

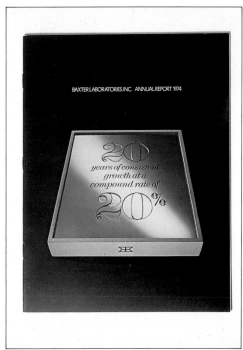

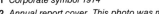

6

6 *Signage, corporate headquarters*
7 *Report binder*
8 *Report spread*
9 *Trial photo for report*
10 *Line print symbol application*
11 *Shipping carton*
12 *Label design*
13 *Model, Signage Design*

25

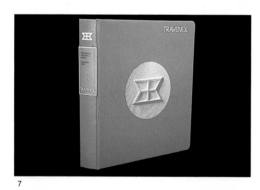

7

8

9

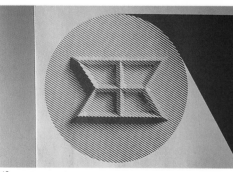

10

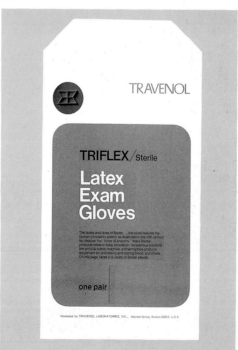

TRAVENOL

TRIFLEX / Sterile

Latex
Exam
Gloves

one pair

12

13

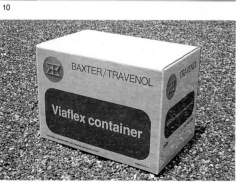

BAXTER/TRAVENOL

Viaflex container

11

1

2

7-UP "See the Light"!

Design for 7-UP was a most enjoyable adventure. My direct client at the company was Orville Roesch, Marketing Director, who was brim-filled with imagination and exciting ideas. Side-by-side was Bob Taylor, Art Director at J. Walter Thompson, who with Roesch, was responsible for the visuals, ads, posters and graphics of "UNCOLA" and "SEE THE LIGHT" slogans which gave 7-UP its exotic and special image over the years I served the company.

It was the "SEE THE LIGHT" slogan that began our search for a whole new image for 7-UP, packaging, graphics and finally corporate I.D. Searching for a graphic idea, I decided that a simulated sign of a grid of lights would become the basis for the program.
The logotype, the package, the signs, graphics and collateral would be based on this grid of dots.
In fact, the commercial film I designed for television advertising was also set to this discipline and the entire 30-second spot was created by animating this grid of dots in color.

26

To present my plan to management, I asked a local photographer, Lef Steinwohl, to help me experiment with this "Light" subject and the name was streaked, strobed and moved in a dark space with an open camera lens. It truly became a study in light and my clients responded favorably.

There were many superb graphic artists who were involved in developing the spirit of the 7-UP product, but it was really Roesch and Taylor who were the leaders into this fantasy project.

1   *7-UP logotype*
2   *Bottle carriers*
3   *Sign design*
4   *Billboard illustration*
5   *Bottle labeling*
6   *Can designs*
7   *Letterhead*
8   *Exploratory photo of logotype*
9   *Image from film*
10 *Ad using can design*
11 *12 pack design*
12-13 *Cargo carriers*

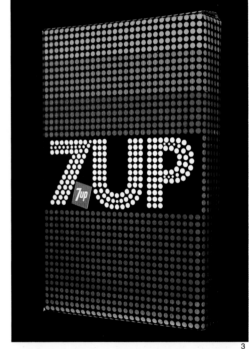

3

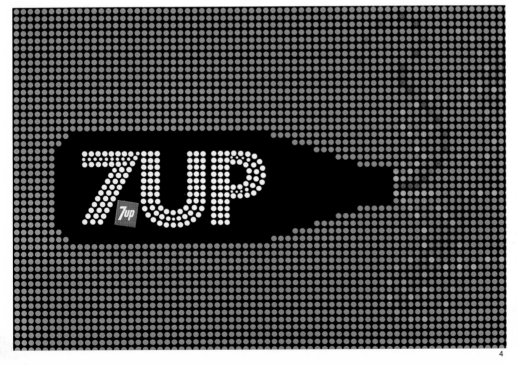

4

5

6

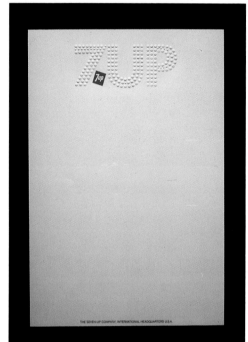

7

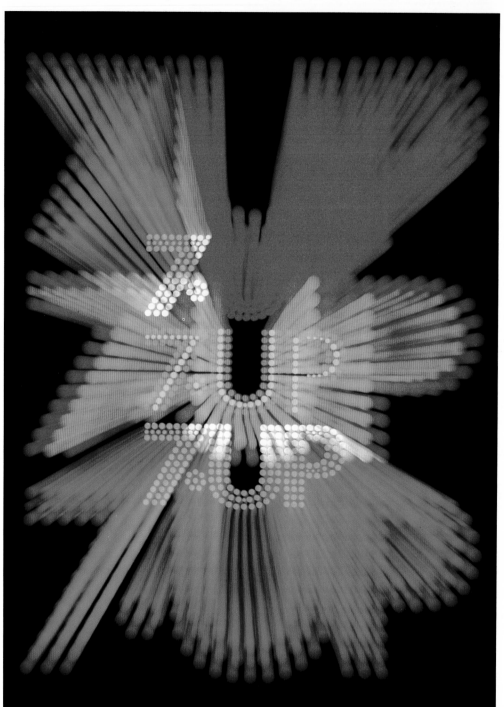

8

9

10

ouverture (fond rouge brun), dépliant devant avec feuilles intérieur et trois feuilles
n couleur. La découverte en carton résultout relle la baille, les feuilles sont empreintes
vitalité. Élément de décoration en finition des légumes en fraix fuatlon des producteurs
on Californie. Au verso de chaque feuille polychrome on trouve des informations cro-
s figures et lignes hodes. (USA)
deux doubles pages tableur d'un catalogue des multiples holidat. pelacement sur des
is et des hacotés. (USA)
et de publicité en faveur de 7-Up; il fait partie d'un portfolio outapromotionnel du
fie Robert Cotton. (USA)

Bookle
Prospe
Broch:

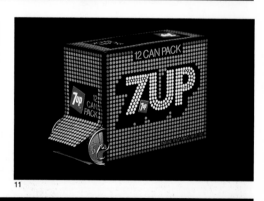

11

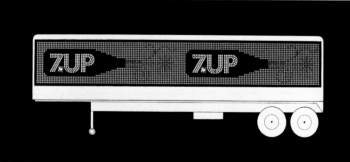

12

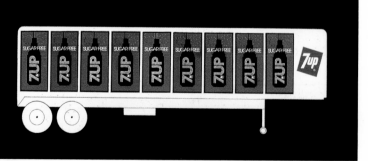

13

BRACH'S CANDIES

My first project for Brach's Candies was
simply to design the packages.
I did not like the dark brown trademark then in
existence and decided to develop a new
design to show to my client, Frank Brach,
Chief Executive and head of the Company.

The design was a series of stripes in sweet
colors, cerise and purple on which
sans serif caps were reversed in white.
Instead of an apostrophe, I decided
on a classic flower form in bright yellow
to replace it. The effect was stunning and a
strong identification for the product.

I presented my designs to Mr. Brach. He said,
"Morton, I like the colors, but I will not change
my trademark." I left the packages and
asked him to leave them on his desk.
He did and two weeks later he called
and told me he agreed to the new design.
It was really a victory for the company.
After 23 years, Brach's still has the
strongest, most recognizable trademark in the
candy marketplace. Even in other colors,
the stripes and flower are persistent.

28

1 Brach's trademark – 1960
2 Christmas package
3 Mass display
4 Candy wraps using the segmented stripe
  in another way
5 "Off-the-shelf" packages

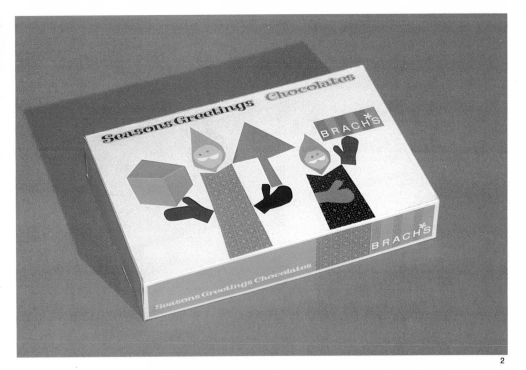

FOULDS

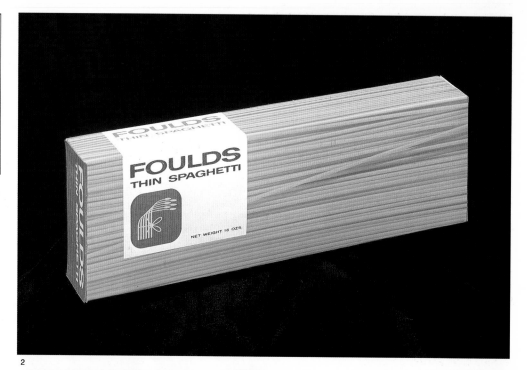

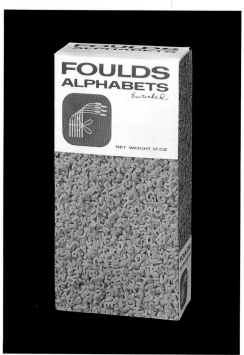

FOULDS: A PRODUCT STORY

The pasta foods of the world are among the most attractive visually. These wheat products generally are quite appealing and pasta makers create a great variety of interesting shapes. Macaroni, spaghetti and shells are only a few of the dozens of shapes and colors that are sold. Set on a photographer's table and in closeups, these types of food positively glow with health and nutrition.

It was this look that lead me to the design of a "see through" package. The food was lit and photographed exactly as it might appear on the shelf under a transparent pack.

The trademark, designed with my associate, John Weber, represented a sheaf of grain blowing in the wind and tied so as to represent the "F" initial.

1 *Foulds trademark – 1963*
  (with John Weber)
2 *Spaghetti package*
3 *Alphabets package*
4 *Mass display*
5 *Mostaccioli package*

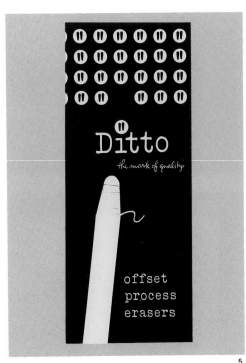

BRUNSWICK CORPORATION

This company asked me to design a new
corporate symbol and signage to
broaden its image.

The need was to identify the organization more
clearly as a diversified major company
with operating divisions in recreational sports,
vehicles, and medical categories.

30

1 *The corporate mark – 1972*
2 *Signage at Corporate Headquarters*
3 *Projected spectacular highway sign*

DITTO CORPORATION

The familiar Ditto mark needed revitalizing.
Our assignment was to design a series
of new packages. In the process, a new
logotype seemed necessary and it was
designed more in keeping with the
market Ditto served,
namely the office supply store, and the
work process it serviced, to duplicate letters,
business forms and data.

4 *Ditto trademark – 1961*
5 *Erasers Package*
6 *Process Fluid Package*
7 *Offset mats Package*

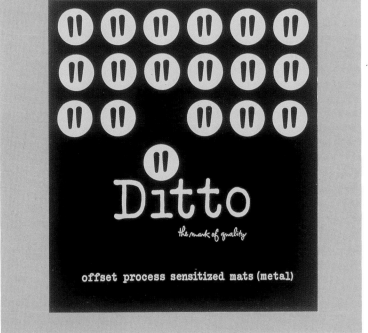

BAUER & BLACK

A division of the Kendall Company,
Bauer & Black had a long history of fine
elastic goods products. The package designs
were created to give these
products two new values.
The first, design to fit the contemporary
drug store arena and to meet competition.
Second, self-service was necessary and
a whole new system of information evolved.
A new product, "Affection", a germicidal lotion,
needed a package and display.
The plastic package which we invented
was required to dispense 1 c.c. of liquid and
the grips at the top did exactly that
when squeezed once.

1 *Bauer & Black trademark – 1959*
2 *Package for support hose*
3 *Major line for Elastic goods*
4 *Exploratory graphics*
5 *Package and display for Affection Lotion*

1

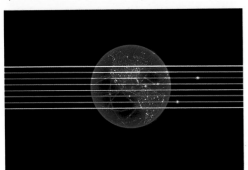

2

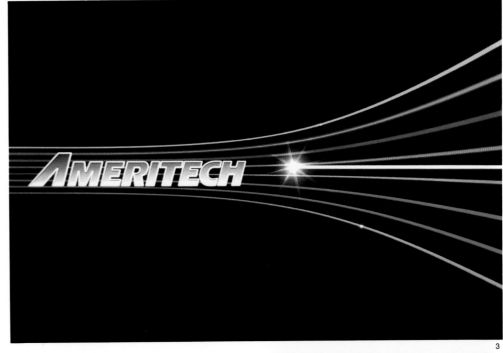

3

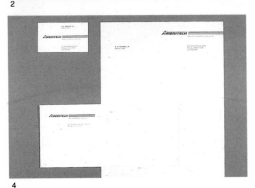

4

5

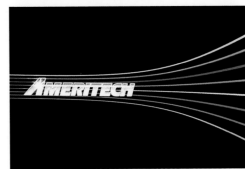

6

7

8

9

10

11

IN A FLASH OF LIGHT

Ameritech, the midwest company divested from AT&T, is a major corporation which has many operating divisions.
The telephone companies in five states surrounding the Great Lakes are among them.

In 1984, we undertook to aid in the development of the corporate name and the design of a symbol that indicates the role the company plays in communication and the transmission of data through its new digital network.

The central design theme revolves around the logotype through which a line of light passes, representing the new optic fiber technologies. At the end a flash of light creates a starburst. This example, one of many applications we have designed, typifies the use of this imagery in print, advertising and film.

The program, deserving a more descriptive book and an enlarged presentation, is currently evolving.

1 *Ameritech trademark*
2 *A series of film images to demonstrate the use of the line of light in the trademark*
3 *Frame from a film production*
4 *Application to stationery*
5 *First use of the trademark in announcement ad*
6 *Frame from a film production*
7 *The mark is completed*
8 *Uses of the mark in advertising*
9 *Star bursting in film*
10 *Corporate headquarters signage*
11 *Final film frame*

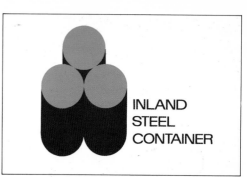

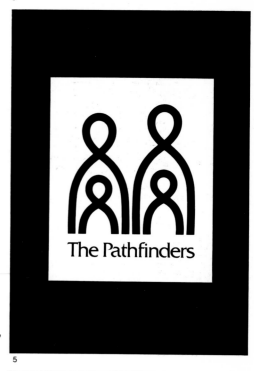

SYMBOLS & BRANDMARKS I

Over the years, I have designed many symbols.
Some were for corporate use, others were
merely brandmarks for their products.
On occasion the brandmark was more important
to the company than the corporate name,
since it identified the company's leading
product, the "Cash Cow" as it were.

Also there were special symbols for associations,
for government agencies and major events
that needed to establish a theme style.

1 *Storkline Furniture trademark – 1964*
2 *Children's furniture, designed for Storkline*
3 *Inland Steel Container trademark – 1976*
4 *Graham Plating Company symbol – 1980
(with Bonnie Bluestein)*
5 *Symbol for "The Path Finders", a population
control group – 1970*
6 *LaSalle Steel Symbol*
7 *Graham Plating Company facilities brochure*
8 *Stone Container Corporation logotype*
9 *Scholastics Books, Symbol*
10 *Proposed design for "Childview" – 1978
Television programs for children*

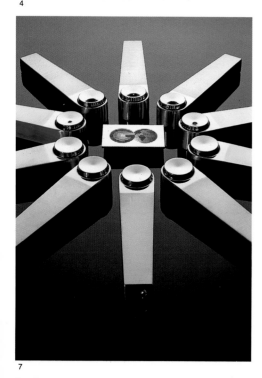

1

2

3

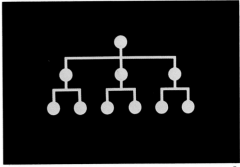

4

SYMBOLS & BRANDMARKS II

Designing symbols for identification requires intense study and discipline.
It is necessary to reach the essence of the company, product or process to be titled.
It is also necessary, in my vocabulary of design, to find the meaning, the core essence of the symbol, trademark or logotype being designed.

Abstract symbols abound. There are some designers who have collections of reject symbols in their files which can be offered again and again simply because they are interesting or unique as visual devices.

There is no way I can offer previous designs to a new client. The value of design is like art — it must be original and true to the need of the design.
If one values meaning as I do, it is necessary to try to symbolize the spirit, work, processes, history, dynamism, tradition or personality of the client or product.

34

1 *ACCO trademark – 1973*
2 *Product package design*
3 *ACCO trucks*
4 *Typical ACCO package*
5 *Trademark, Spencer R. Stuart Associates – 1962, for a management recruiting firm*
6 *Stokley Van Camp trademark*
7 *Signage for Stokely Van Camp*
8 *Stokely truck design*
9 *Brochures, Spencer R. Stuart*
10 *InveQuest trademark – 1980 (with Bonnie Bluestein)*
11 *InveQuest symbols for four divisions*
12 *InveQuest stationery*

5

7

6

8

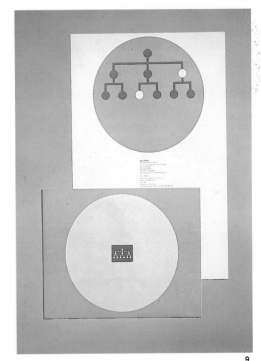

9

10

11

12

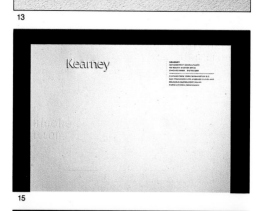

13

FraternaLife Insurance

Aid Association for Lutherans

14

A loaf of bread, a jug of soda pop & we

16

15

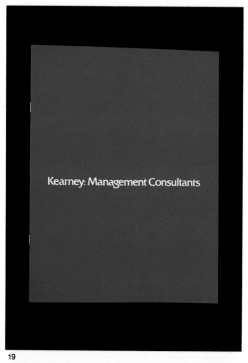

17

13 *Kearney trademark – 1976, for a management consulting group*

14 *Aid Association for Lutherans trademark – 1970*

15 *Kearney Stationery*

16 *Aid Association trademark applied to advertising*

17 *Kearney stationery*

18 *General American Transportation (GATX)*

19 *Kearney brochure*

20 *GATX tank car*

21 *Slipcase and brochures*

22 *Proposed, Rath Packing Company 1970*

23 *Symbol, heart risk research 1974 (with John Weber)*

GATX

18

Kearney: Management Consultants

19

20

21

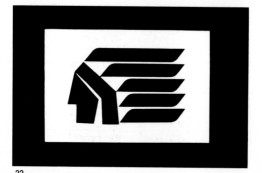

22

MRFIT

23

A UNIQUE FESTIVAL

In 1985 I was asked to establish the visual
symbolism and set the tone for
the first Chicago International Theatre Festival.
My clients were Jane and Bernie Sahlins,
then owners, founders and directors
of Second City, a world famous comedy and
improvisational theater.
We had previously designed the new
logotype and made a television
commercial for them.

This was a grand opportunity to capture the
flavors of many countries, actors groups and
staging from around the world.
It needed a classic theme
and in my usual mode, I considered the
design for a long time.
I read books on the Theater, talked to
Jane, listened and scratched ideas.
A sentence I read elsewhere struck a chord.
William Faulkner said, "Everyone writes
behind a mask." This translated to my project,
"The mask is the universal symbol of the
theater. It is the mask of all of life."

This then became the colorful symbol of the
festival. It was implanted on everything
printed, banners, buttons, tickets
and brochures. The colors and minor patterns
were designed to symbolize world flags.

The lettering was done by my associate,
John Weber, master calligrapher.

3

4

5

1 Symbol for festival – 1985
2 Brochures, invitations and stationery
3 Program and festival books, mask and buttons
  for festival personnel
4 Poster design
5 Concept sketches

GRAPHICS

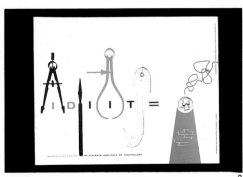

Since my earliest moment of awareness
I loved graphics. My pictures pleased my
parents, my teachers and my friends.
Drawing was always easy and carrying that
sense of art into design was simple.

I could sketch, render, illustrate my designs
and the excitement of graphics
was all-consuming.
The elements of design were quite easy to fulfill.
The meaning of design was not.
Design needs intellectual application to get the
reader to understand and respond.

Graphics are the backbone of design. There are
more graphics designers at work than any
other kind. And graphics can be applied to
everything that needs communicating.

We can apply our graphics to pages, packaging,
signs, products, billboards, posters, vehicles,
uniforms, books, even money and we can
enhance or demean the image.

If I were pinned down to have to describe
the one area of design that I really represent,
I would have to choose graphic design.

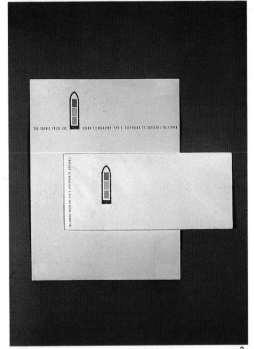

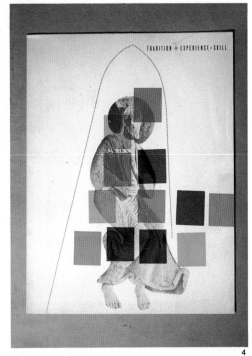

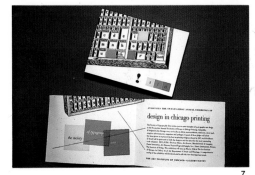

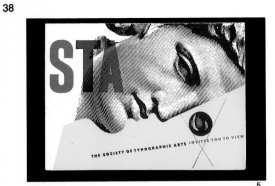

1 *Christmas card*
2 *Brochure for the Institute of Design, IIT, 1950*
3 *Letterheads for Gothic Press, 1952*
4 *Brochure for Gothic Press, 1952*
5-6-7 *Folders for the Society of Typographic Arts, 1956*
8 *Folder for R.R. Donelley, Printers*
9 *Poster design as a momento, distributed on
    our STA trip to China*
10 *Design for Report Brochure, Aspen Design Conference,
    1958*

11

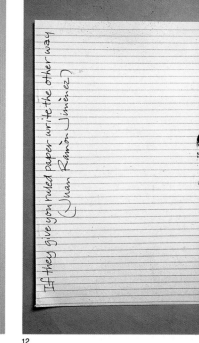

12

13

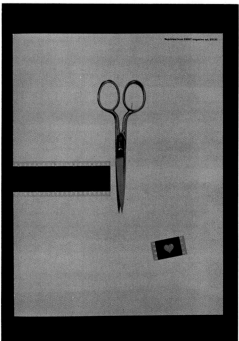

14

11 *Record album cover design for Life Magazine, containing music from our film for promoting the magazine, 1960*

12 *Cover for Print Magazine*

13 *Menu design for an experimental Brunswick Bowling Alley, 1955*

14 *Self promotion for our films, 1962*

15 *Catalog for AD gallery exhibit of my work, 1950*

16 *Invitations to an exhibition of our work designed with Susan Jackson Keig, associate*

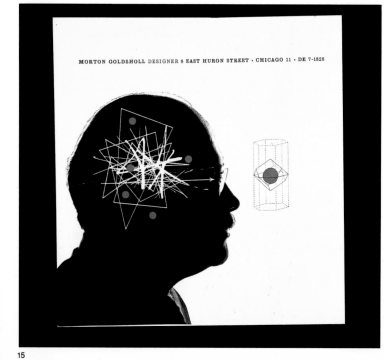

15

16

GRAPHICS

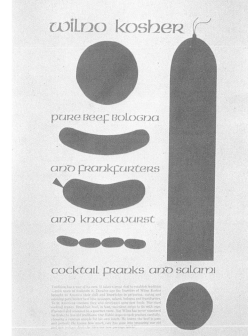

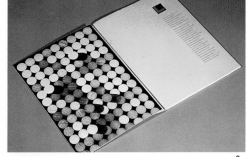

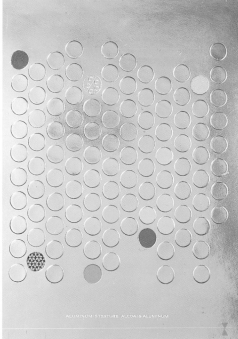

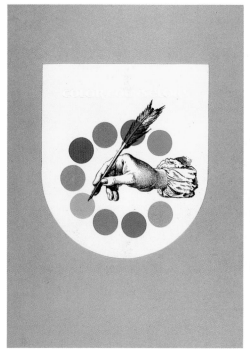

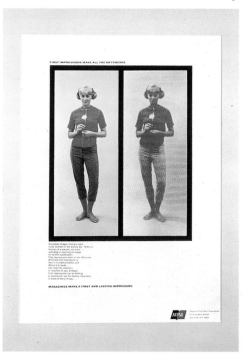

There were many graphic projects for a great
variety of subjects, some for industry,
some for the design groups I belonged to,
others for design periodicals,
many ''free'' design assignments that were
always interesting to do.

1 *Advertisment design for Alcoa Foil*
2 *Advertisement for delicatessen products*
3 *Brochure for LaSalle Steel*
4 *Packaging exhibition catalog for AIGA*
5 *Design mark for a color counselling service*
6 *Photo illustration for LaSalle Steel*
7 *Advertisement for Magazine Publishers Association*

8

9

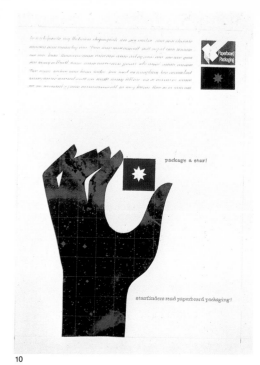

10

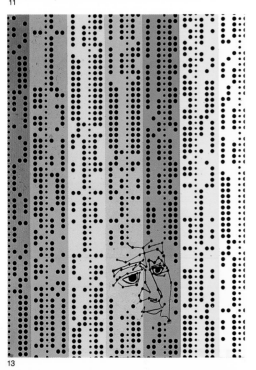

11

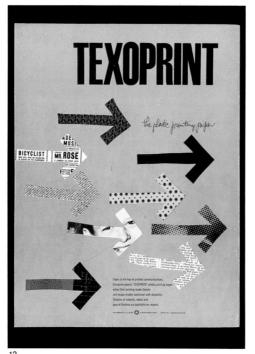

12

41

13

14

15

42

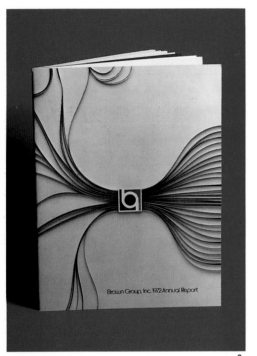

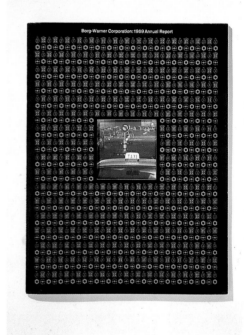

1 Annual Report Cover for The Brown Group
2 Helene Curtis Annual Report
3 Brown Group Annual Report
4 Borg-Warner Annual Report
5 Front and back covers Brown Group Report
6 Inside spread Brown Group Report
7 Cover design for film group brochure
8 Cover for Kimberly-Clark Annual Report

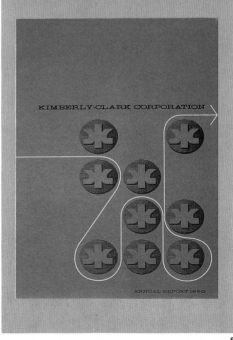

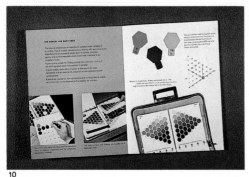

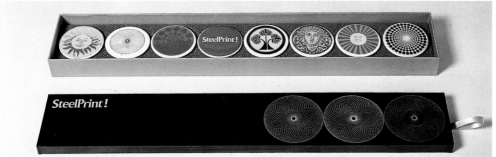

43

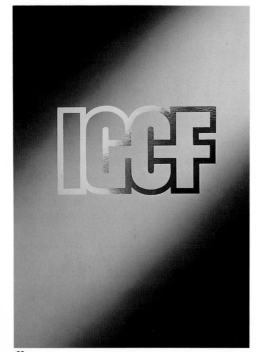

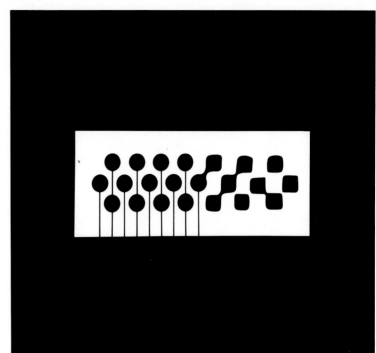

1

2

44

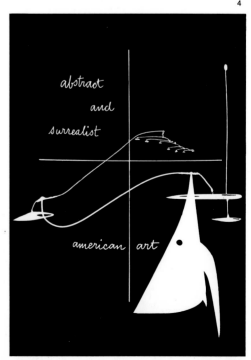

OASIS RESTAURANTS

3

REHABILITATION INSTITUTE OF CHICAGO

4

5

abstract
and
surrealist

american art

6

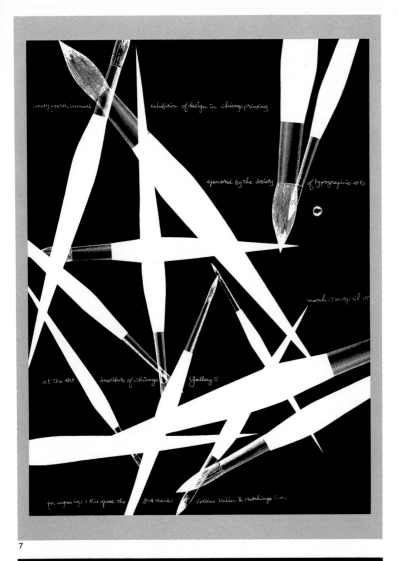

7

1 *Symbol design for Peace Corps*
2 *Graphics for Kimberly Clark Munising Bond*
3 *Graphics for tollway oasis restaurants*
4 *Graphic symbol for Chicago Rehabilitation Center*
5 *Proposed graphics for Childview Productions*
6 *Catalog of Abstract & Surrealist Art
  in America Exhibition*
7 *Society of Typographic Arts announcement
  advertisement*
8 *Poster design for Industrial Designers Society
  of America*
9 *Men's store ad for Marshall Field's – 1955*

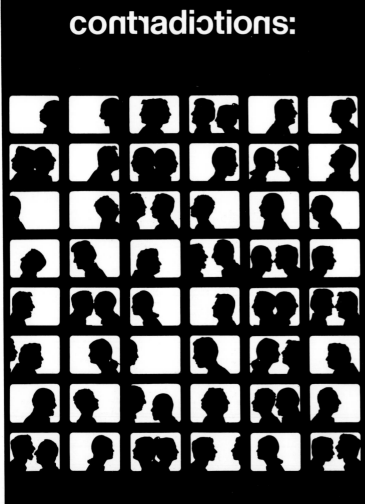

8

9

PACKAGING DESIGN

1

2

3

The package is more than a selling device. It does that. But its first duty is to protect the product from breakage, rain, cold, heat, stacking and other assorted abuses, insects and vandals, from the moment of its manufacture through shipping and storage until it reaches the consumer.

And if it is well designed it will also be easy to open, reseal and simple to dispose of. Quite a task for what is often only a thin plastic film or a flimsy piece of chipboard.

Design for packaging is a special and worthy task.

My first job was in a packaging plant and I was assigned all the creative and production tasks including directing the die cutting and printing processes. Even today all the package designs we do are constructed in the studio as mockups. It is necessary for us to know all the steps involved in producing it as well as recognize all the needs of the user. Packaging design is design for use.

And it definitely includes design to attract and accurately inform the consumer. The best motive for repeat sales in is the product itself. The graphic design can only "sell" the product once. If that sale includes misinformation that deceives the buyer, there will be no repeat sales and, soon, no product being sold.

46

4

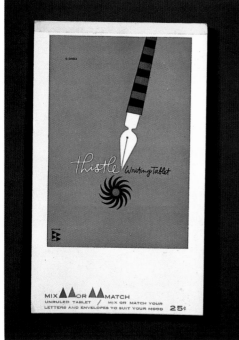

5

6

7

8

9

10

11

1 *Package for materials 1945*
2 *Parlux package 1946*
3 *Lighter Fluid package 1946*
4 *Bakery and confectionery packaging 1949*
5 *Stationery design 1950*
6 *Stationery design 1950*
7 *Candy and confectionery 1949*
8 *Candy packaging 1949*
9 *Hair products packaging 1952*
10 *Cereal packaging 1955*
11 *Ice cream container 1958*
12 *Photographic products shipping container 1962*
13 *Candy packaging 1960*

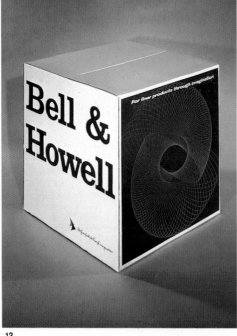

12

13

QUAKER PACKAGE DESIGN

For many years I worked for the Quaker Oats Company on cereal and special products design.

Part of this time I worked with Max Lomont, Director of Design, Grocery Products, and together we created many unique product packages and special graphics. We also redesigned the Aunt Jemima trademark to bring it up to a more current visual theme and standardization.

48

1 *Special brand symbol*

2 *Package design that included a major research study to develop a very successful new product.*

3 *Second flavor for the cereal*

4-7 *Trial graphic designs for research to test early traditional forms*

8 *Package mockups for traditional forms*

9 *Special promotional collection of old Quaker labels from the 1800's to use in the design of special tins*

10 *Natural grain packages*

11 *Detail of grain packs*

12 *Experimental plastic cover for candy bars to emphasize a crunchy product*

13 *Close up of molded forms*

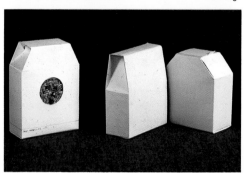

9

10

11

49

12

13

BRUCE WAX AND CLEANERS

This package design assignment was created to clearly define the quality of Bruce products which were produced and marketed by a major flooring manufacturer.
One of the objectives was to clarify the correct uses of the products specifically for wood or tile floors. The decision was made to develop graphics that were unmistakable.

50

1 *First concept comprehensives*
2 *Special Blow Mold plastic container design*
3 *Cleaning Wax gallon, quart and pint for wood floors*
4 *Plastic package design*
5 *Product line*
6 *Floor tile packages*

1

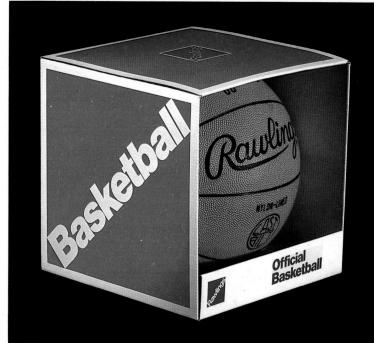

2

RAWLINGS

3

4

1 *Baseball glove package*
2 *Basketball package*
3 *Helmet package*
4 *Golf ball counter package*
5 *Baseball counter display*
6 *Hockey helmet package*
7 *Top quality golf ball set*
8 *Closeup of golf ball container designed with Jim Neill, associate*

5

6

51

7

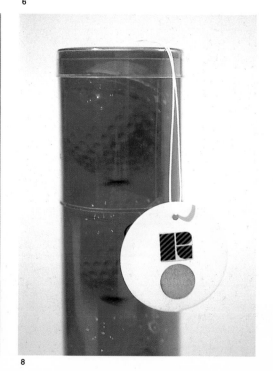

8

1. There were many trials for Kleenex Table Napkins. This package was planned for elegant embossed dinner napkins.

2. In contrast, this design was planned for bulk, commodity type napkins.

3. Many napkin packages assumed odd shapes.

4. One interesting program included this counter top display of craft colors for Illinois Bronze which has an extensive line of such products.

5. Exploratory packages for foil were developed for market testing.

6. A total line of products for this Tornado Brand of propane gas containers were designed around this symbol.

52

7. This series of "Wet-Dry" wipes were designed to carry about in travels. The package was explored in cardboard and then molded into a plastic form.

8-9. Two paint packages for Montgomery Ward, part of an extensive line. "Storm Coat" was designed with Wendy Pressley-Jacobs, an associate.

10. The Wet-Dry pack in development stage

11. The Wet-Dry pack in development stage

12. The final package

13. The general Country Colors Craft Paint line

14. Stock container for Automotive Gears for Perfection American Gear Company

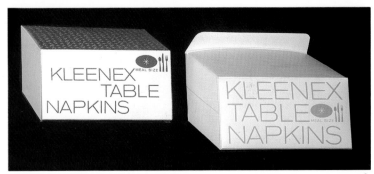

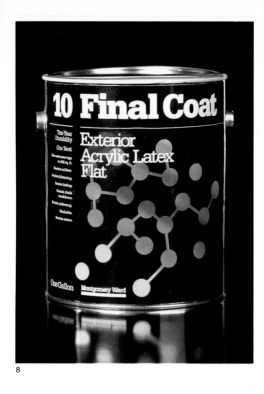

8

9

7

10

11

53

13

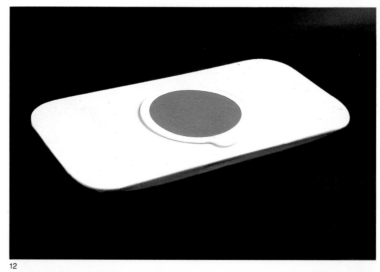

12

14

1 *Design for Town House Crackers showing a design approach to the layout of the product photography.*

2 *Morningstar Trademark for TVP products designed for Miles Laboratories. This product is created from vegetable products and the ''carved'' farm scene implied the source. This was designed with John Weber, who carved the rough mockup which was then sculpted by a wood carver.*

3 *Use of the symbol on an extensive line of products*

4 *Logotype for Pasta Products*

5 *Package design for Pasta Products*

6 *Schlitz Malt Liquor packaging was a first use by a major can supplier to lithograph and emboss the can in line on the same equipment*

7 *Proposed bottle design which used ruby colored glass, evidently to extend the vitality and shelf life of the product*

8 *Six packs and mass display*

54

1

2

3

4

5

PACKAGING

1

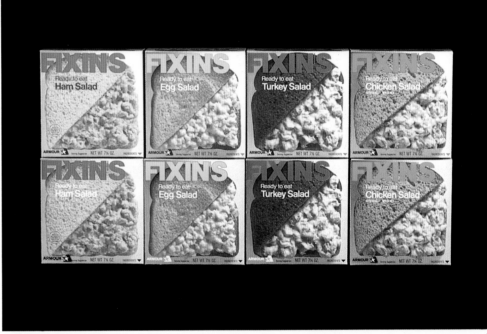

2

1 Frankfurter packaging for Vienna Sausage, one of many created for the company since 1956

2 Proposed packages for sandwich spread products for Armour. This was designed with Jim Neill, associate.

3 Hi-C cans and bottles were redesigned to enhance the appeal. These orange fruit drinks were designed to show the content rather than the previous package which had pictures of children drinking the product.

4 Hi-C in large cans showing the variety

5 Eggs were the important ingredient in the noodles and the symbol and package projected that.

6 Design for a soft drink for the Seven-Up Company

7 Design for a gourmet series of grocery products

8 Frozen food packages for Chun King

9 Proposed design for Stokely Van Camp

10 Cheesecake package designs for Pie Piper. The packages were often displayed together and formed one larger cake image

11 Proposed design for Chun King Chinese food

56

3

4

6

5

7

8

9

57

10

11

LIGHT/PHOTOGRAPHY/FILM

When Moholy-Nagy spoke of light in terms of the new artists he became lyrical in his description. He was intrigued with photography and its uses in graphics and film.
He thoroughly infected his students and wrote at length in all his books on the magic and the fantasy of this new medium.

I was and remain a photographer
in a broad sense.

The magic of the emerging print in a darkroom tray has intrigued me from the beginning. However, thousands of slides that documented trips and people soon became mundane to me. As a result of Moholy's urging, I turned to experiments seeking the purest forms of color in light and searching for optics and lenses of strange conformations to bend, twist and scatter light onto film.

This curiosity remains. The acuity of the camera lens has warped my willingness to accept videotape and its characteristic texture as a final true image.

The film, which Moholy described as "The Art of this Century" remains the challenge of my life as a designer.
I am aware of the power of film and how it reaches people.
The world has responded to this medium just as Moholy predicted.

In the section following I wish to call your attention to the fact that film is a communal art. There are many involved in the shooting crews, in editing and post production. I can only claim having a major control of the design, concept and direction. On rare occasions I also did the photography. Quite often I wrote the script since this aspect creates the film structure.

Film as a subject deserves a book of its own and my full attention.
But for now, I hope that this book can serve to inspire designers to also study and work in this continuously fascinating medium.

58

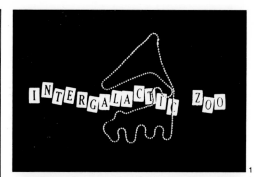

1

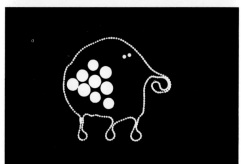

2

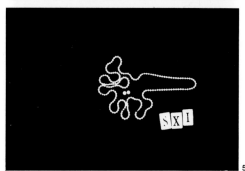

3

4

5

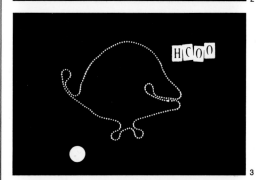

6

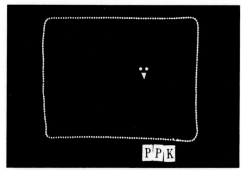

7

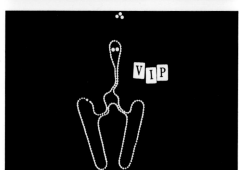

8

9

needless to say, the last animal "Zuman" is now extinct.

INTERGALACTIC ETHNOLOGICAL SOCIETY

10

This four minute film was my first try at animation. It was completed in one 8 hour day. A simple beaded chain was moved slightly for each frame. The idea for the film evolved spontaneously and I "named" each animal in the zoo as they were created. It was made in 1958.

1

2

3

4

5

6

7

8

9

10

11

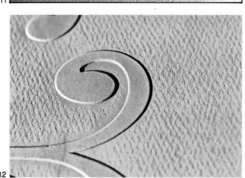

12

13

14

15

16

PAPER: THE PROLOGUE

Borrowing a theme from Shakespeare who wrote, "The past is prologue" is what inspired this film on America's finest paper, cover and text papers. It was produced for the American Paper Institute in Washington, D.C. for 40 paper manufacturers who produce these materials.

Intended as a showpiece, the film presents the texture, colors, printability, flexibility in use, permanence and beauty of these papers.

The objective was to emphasize the tactile sense and hand feel of these papers as they were used in greeting cards, annual reports, elegant books, brochures and beautifully designed special pieces.

Opening with a history of paper filmed at the Dard Hunter Paper Museum in the Institute of Paper Chemistry in Appleton, Wisconsin, USA, the film explores the uses of paper throughout our society, art and culture.

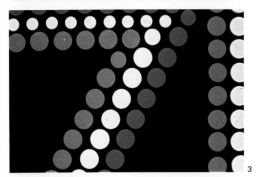

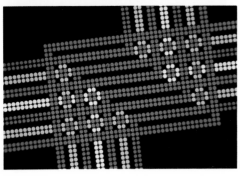

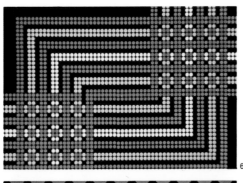

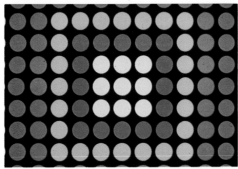

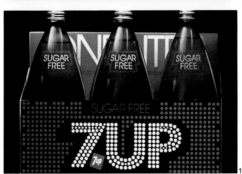

60

SEVEN-UP

This commercial was designed with the discipline of the dot grid superimposed on the corporate design program. Animated to deliver the message of Sugar-free 7UP, the transforming images created the illusion of a sign made of electric lights. All of this was animated to a percussive music track.

VO-5

One of the first commercials I did was for VO-5 Hair Dressing. Still shots of the models were intercut with enlargements of the name and appeared in the negative spaces. The percussive editing related to vibrant music.

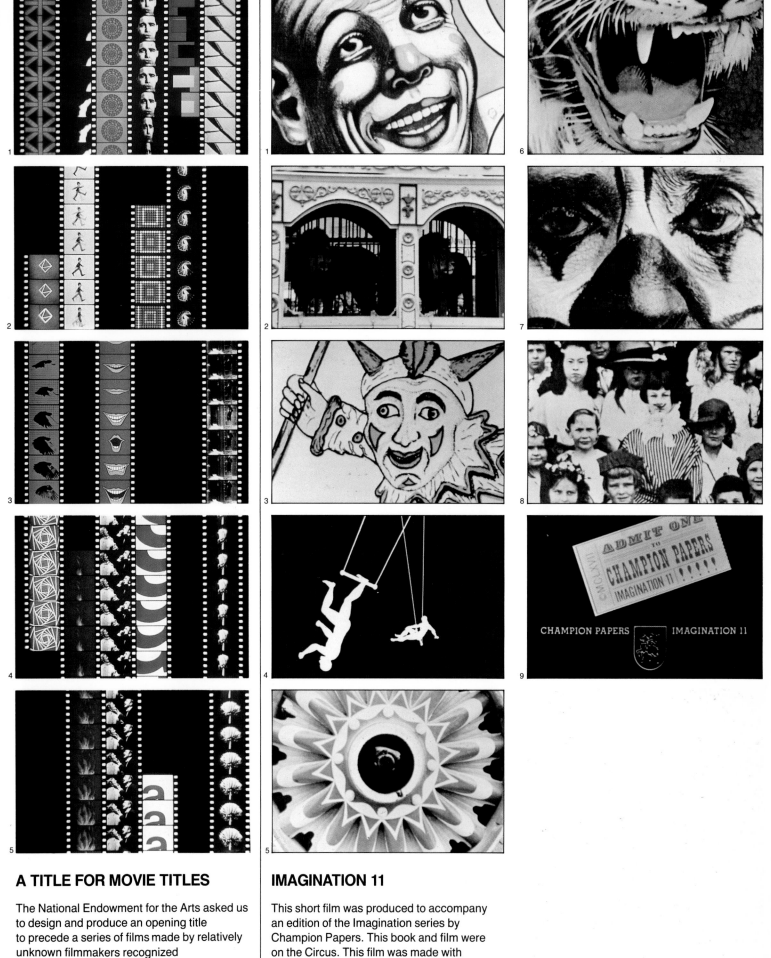

A TITLE FOR MOVIE TITLES

The National Endowment for the Arts asked us
to design and produce an opening title
to precede a series of films made by relatively
unknown filmmakers recognized
only by cinema clubs.

The film uses many types of images on running
strips represented by the sprocket holes.
This film was made with Paul Jessel,
our Director of Animation.

IMAGINATION 11

This short film was produced to accompany
an edition of the Imagination series by
Champion Papers. This book and film were
on the Circus. This film was made with
Wayne Boyer and Larry Janiak, our associates.

62

YES WE CAN!

A 30-second, full animation commercial produced for Kellogg cereals was intended to celebrate the U.S. Bicentennial. It was created in collaboration with Ken Mundie, who directed the film and animated it with Paul Jessel and our staff.

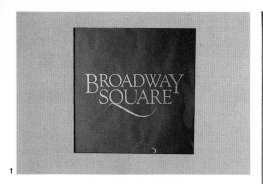

1

1

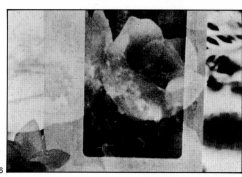

6

2

2

7

3

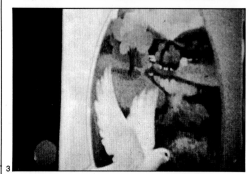

3

8

63

4

4

9

5

5

BROADWAY SQUARE

This short animated film was really a
stop-motion production made with a cube
constructed to move in all directions.
Each side was illustrated with paper
sculptures and on one face with actual
animation cels to animate a fountain design.
The film announced a new shopping mall.
It was animated by Pete Dakis, a staff member.
Artwork was by John Weber.

HALLMARK

As a result of my film for cover and text
papers, the sequence on greeting cards
caught the eye of Hallmark cards.
They gave us two commercials to do on their
fine paper products for each special
television show they broadcast for a period of
4 years. The above commercial was on the
celebration of Easter.

1

2

3

4

5

1

2

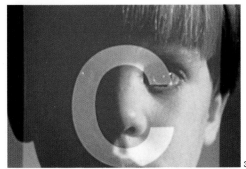

3

4

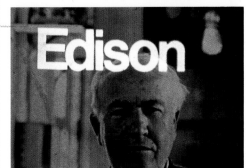

5

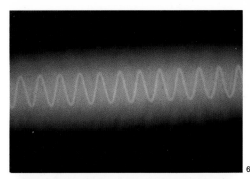

6

7

8

9

REVLON

The quantized image shown was created by a
unique lens system, an array of lenses
that flattened each photographic tone into
a pure square of color.
The Revlon commercial was its first use
in television advertising. It was produced
for Revlon through Leo Burnett Advertising.
The conversions were by Harry Goldsholl.

ABC

This short film was used as a title for
the films in the Commonwealth Edison
Company Library. It was also converted
into a 60-second commercial.

The purpose was to inform the audience as to
their services and concerns
for the many public uses of energy and the
thousands of Edison people who are involved.
It was created with Millie Goldsholl.

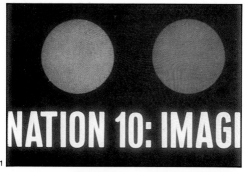

IMAGINATION 10

A documentary film on the inner life of the railroad produced for the Champion Paper Company.

The film was issued in conjunction with the 10th edition of the Imagination series of brochures which dealt with the use of paper by the railroads and some of these graphics are included in the footage.

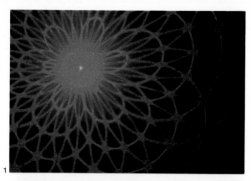

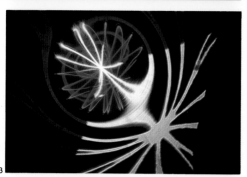

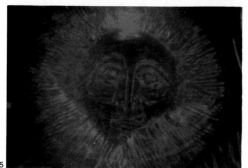

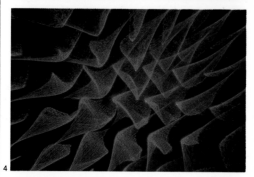

POPTIC

A short film based on my optical experiments and some of the results obtained by penetrating the "Star" of the lens with graphic images.
I call them Light Rosettes,
first published in IDEA magazine,
a Japanese publication.

1

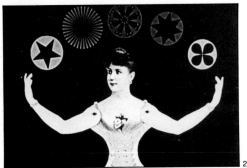

2

3

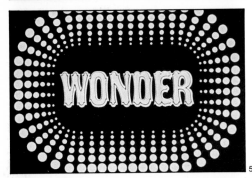

4

5

6

66

1

2

3

4

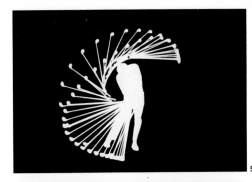

5

6

7

8

GOLF STROBE

This title, also for Mr. Schwimmer, was made by
photographing a golfer in clear silhouette
and, using 90 positions of the club itself,
creating a strobelike recording of a golf swing.
This meant that the single
strip of film passed through the animation
camera 90 times. Bill Langdon
was the staff animator.

WONDER CIRCUS

This film title was created for Walt Schwimmer
Productions and created with graphics
and live action filming of circus life
and events. It was done
in conjunction with Ed Bedno, a staff member.

READING: A GIFT FOR LIFE

1

2

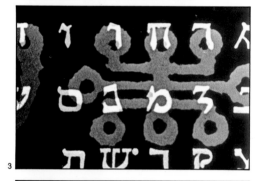

3

4

5

6

7

8

9

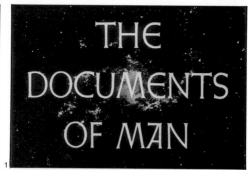

1

2

3

4

5

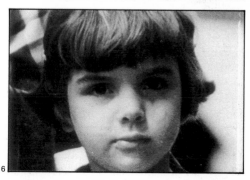

6

67

READING: A GIFT OF LIFE

This was a film created to demonstrate the
value of a special reading system
developed by Scott Foresman, publishers
of educational materials and books.
The film was related closely to the system and
also demonstrated reading
situations with children.

THE DOCUMENTS OF MAN

A documentary presenting the work and history
of the Aid Association for Lutherans.
The benevolent and fraternal work
of the society is explored in detail.
This film uses animation and live action.

PHOTOGRAPHY AND DESIGN

In the beginning photography had limited goals. Since early photographs were made with primitive materials and processes, long exposure times forced the photographers into shooting stilted portraits or inanimate objects.

It was the enoromous strides in photo-technology that freed the photographer and helped to make photography into an art. And it was the artist that finally brought it to fruition.

Moholy established a goal that intrigued his students and forever after a camera and film was always at hand.

But what is photography? It's new freedom, fast lenses, exotic camera mechanisms, infinite varieties of film, instantaneous prints, incredible recordings of the unseen micro and macro worlds, limitless new landscapes in space and the sea, all point to Moholy's prediction that the pursuit of light and shadow would capture the imagination of all human beings, unskilled or sophisticated. Everyone enjoys a picture.

The designer is especially sensitive to photography which has become an integral part of design. And the curious designer/photographer considers the camera as a new tool, to create new images, to extend art into new dimensions, to find visuals that never existed in life and to capture living things in a new way so as to broaden our awareness of the nature of the world of humans, animals and plants.

Probably the greatest value of photography may be that it has become a people's art, Moholy also said "in the future, children will have crayons in one hand and cameras in the other" and it is true.

The extension of the still picture into film and videography has long been recognized. Muybridge is called the father of motion pictures.
And Moholy would have smiled and enjoyed the ease with which children can now make video-productions, shooting, editing and recording sound.

I have made photographs for 55 years and I never was a "photographer". This is indicative of all the processes I had to learn to become a designer/film maker. And I "use" all of them as necessary.

I always enjoyed playing with new forms of light and found the star of a lens could be manipulated; that lenses could be arranged in arrays for multiple images; virtual volume could be created to record motion and that motion could be chopped into strobing fragments; that images could be quantized into squares of pure color and reformed into new images that resembled paintings and tapestries.

I could pursue a grandchild to film a precious moment of young energy or a clumsy handling of eye glasses. There are flowers to record at peak, fragile moments and macro details to find and enlarge.

And there is also the poetry of the landscape over the world, exotic countries and people to explore and remember.

Photography and design is inseparable. What would printing be without photography?

I believe it is not too far fetched to say that photography and its sister art, film, has changed us.
We can see, in detail, the devastation of war, the archives of a holocaust as well as the celebrations and the joys of mankind. Elections can be won or lost in the blink of an eye and the explosion of a space ship can be shared in horror by millions at once.

68

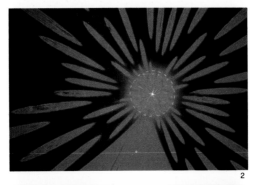

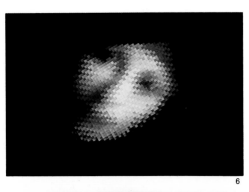

1 *Experimental photo*
2 *Lens Star photo*
3 *Experimental – conversion of painting*
4 *Experiment – circle conversion*
5 *Lens Star photo*
6 *Experimental conversion*
7 *Painting and scratchout on 35mm negative*

69

8 New York scene
9 Flower study
10 Child in airport
11 Flower study
12 Child and glasses
13 Child on shore
14 Industrial photo
15 Japan scene
16 Japan scene
17 Japan scene
18 Japan scene
19 Japan scene

1 *This was taken by Millie in Mexico City.*
2 *This was taken at the same time. The light was just right. This is my favorite picture of Millie. Taken in 1974.*
3 *Our Studio and office.*
4 *Our house. This picture is 34 years old. It remains the same.*
5 *An interior view of the house.*
6 *The Garden.*

Morton Goldsholl lives in Highland Park, Illinois, U.S.A. His home was designed by Millie Goldsholl, his wife, who studied architecture at the School of Design. They have lived there for 35 years. Their Studio is in Northfield, Illinois, about 8 miles from their home. It also was designed by Millie before she turned to making films.

He began as a freelance artist and after two years as a package designer in a carton plant and another two years in an advertising art studio, he reentered freelance. As his assignments grew, he needed assistance and in 1955, ten years later, formed Goldsholl Associates which continued until 1984 when Morton and Millie asked Harry Goldsholl to join them. The current company, Goldsholl Design and Film, consists of three groups; Goldsholl Design Group, Goldsholl Film Group, and Informational Media, which is responsible for the production and distribution of longer films.

Morton and Millie have two children. Harry, who is a partner in the Studio and heads the Film Group, and Gleda Dreke, their daughter who lives with her husband and three children in Wisconsin.

Morton's home has a studio which has many books, collected over 50 years, that relate to design, art, film making, photography, typography, calligraphy and other graphics. The books reflect an international curiosity. They were created in Japan, Germany, Italy, France, among others. He prizes six books that are the original Bauhausbucher, two of which were authored by Moholy. Other series are the large volumes published on the National Treasures of Japan and the entire issue of Graphis from the first edition to the current number.

At least 20% of the books are on science and technology, another area of constant interest. He also collects old iconographic encyclopedias and early Muybridge books on his sequence photography of humans and animals.

Morton and Millie enjoy simple pleasures. The Chicago Botanical Garden is nearby and walks and garden events take them there frequently. He enjoys growing plants. Succulents and tender plants fill their home and garden. Their home environment relates to the garden and outdoors and the seasonal changes have fascinated them both for the entire 35 years of living there.

They both enjoy the theater and films. One recent pleasure was to see all nine plays during the recent Chicago International Theatre Festival. They agreed that the Japanese Company "The Suzuki Company of Toga" that performed "The Trojan Women" was the highlight of the festival.

Recently, Morton said to a group of visitors from Japan, when asked to comment on his work in design and film and his personal philosophy:

"I have mostly enjoyed working in design and film. There have been moments when I felt otherwise. There were disappointments and, in the beginning in the depression years, very lean times.
When I was young searching for work was the major task.

It was a short period however. But "just work" was not satisfactory for too long. Generally, work in a service studio means that an artist must subjugate himself to each mundane task. Retouching photos, keylining and pasteups, ordering type and doing lettering are perfectly useful tasks. But my goals were being shaped and crystallized by Moholy and Kepes and the books and ideas of the Bauhaus.

My satisfaction with just working was soon over and I turned to other things. I began searching for assignments and more difficult tasks. Egbert Jacobson was my savior. He challenged me and I was concerned I could never satisfy that great art director. The Container Corporation image was awesome. Herbert Bayer, Kepes and Herbert Matter were my inspiration and all of them worked for Jacobson.

I must have done my assignments well. They were all accepted and I went on to working for Jake for many years.

There were many awards and much acclaim. Most of these were for specific design projects. The most rewarding of all, however, were the few honors given to me as a person, a whole designer, or recognizing a body of work rather than a specific design.

My first was to be elected President of STA in 1949, a signal honor from one of the finest graphic societies in the world. The Society of Typographic Arts was the first group I ever joined and I got my first award from it, for a letterhead I designed for Haskell Wexler, my friend, a cinematographer and film director, for his first studio.

Another equally great honor was my election in 1964 by the National Society of Art Directors and its membership as the "Art Director of the Year". And yet another, being named the "Packaging Designer of the Year" by the Package Designers Council in 1962 and again in 1978.

These were unforgettable moments. They gave me a deeper sense of security about my work and a new maturity that helped me to make better decisions about my future. I also realized that great as the awards others bestow on one, the greatest satisfaction was still when a new thought and idea that answered the problem occured and that my design, on occasion, fulfilled a real need.

At best, I now believe I have come into a balance. I work the way I live. Yin-Yang. Opposites are not opposites, they are one. The task and the solution, just as day and night, are one. A few years ago I learned I *had* to live on a macrobiotic diet. It was difficult to modify a lifelong habit and mode. Now, I *want* to live on a macrobiotic diet. It is in balance. It has become a model for my life and work. Perhaps it's the way to see all things in continuum.

Design, art, film, writing, speaking and listening, learning and teaching have become one.

Finally, there is a matter that is more difficult to discuss. Personal integrity is no small matter and I have commented on it only when asked. This is strictly personal. I do not preach to others. It is many facetted. It means learning to say yes or no in the face of accepting a questionable project. Making packages *look* bigger by design. Claiming others work for my own or copying a style, an idea or a device simply because it is popular. Demeaning human beings in commercials is one of my special dislikes. Designing anything that will harm others or simply seduce them is another. There is no lasting joy or satisfaction in any of the above even if they win awards or great fortunes.

When I was a small boy my grandfather, who lived to 95, said to me with a twinkle in his eyes: 'If you eat soap for 100 years, you will live a long time.' He smiled while I spit at the thought. Much later, I realized what he meant was, if you write poetry, love or simply listen to the wind for 100 years you will live a long time."

Morton Goldsholl will be 75 in 1986. He says there are many more things to be done to reach 100. He just now said to me, "Forty years are not enough. I want more!"

71

Written by
Morton Goldsholl
August 1, 1986

MORTON GOLDSHOLL,
born in Chicago, December 21, 1911.
Studied and worked in Chicago schools,
studios and industry in 1931.
Spare time study at School of Design
with Moholy-Nagy and George Kepes, 1939.
Freelance office opened, 1941. Formed
Morton Goldsholl Design Associates in 1955.
Elected to Board of Directors, STA, 1948.
Elected president STA, 1949.
Elected Vice President,
International Design Conference, 1957.
Elected Program Chairman, 1959.
Member, STA, AGC, IDI, PDC,
ASID, IFPA and SMPTE.

Active in many professional societies,
Goldsholl has lectured widely in the
United States, Japan, and Canada to university,
design and business groups
and has contributed articles to
numerous journals. His work has been
reproduced in major publications and
exhibited throughout the world.

During the past 40 years, his design
office has been awarded hundreds of citations
in design and film making in
national and international exhibitions.
In 1958, he was named
Honorary Member of the
Society of Typographic Arts.
In 1963, Goldsholl won the coveted
Package Designers Council
"Industry Award of the Year";
in 1964, he was nominated and elected
"Art Director of the Year" by the
National Society of Art Directors,
named an Honorary Member of the
Art Directors Club of Chicago and designated
"Chicago Artist of the Year."
In 1966, he was presented with the
Walter Paepcke Design Award,
which cited the role of the designer
as an important force in American business.
In 1967, he was awarded Best of Show by the
Artists Guild of Chicago for Exphotage
(experimental photography) and
Best of Show in their Annual Exhibit
of Editorial and Advertising Art.
In 1972, he was again named Designer of the
Year by the Package Designers Council.

Awards for graphic, packaging and
product design from STA, AIGA,
Folding Box Association,
Lithographers National Association,
Art Directors Club of Chicago,
Milwaukee and New York, Good Design
Show of Museum of Modern Art,
Architectural and Interior Design selection for
"Interiors of the Year"
by Interiors magazine,
Plastics award from Koppers,
"50 Packages of the Year" by AIGA.
Work and articles published by Graphis,
Modern Packaging, Graphika, Typographica,
Industrial Design, etc.
Exhibition of work in 1950 at A.D. Gallery, N.Y.
Experimental work in Design,
photography and Film.

In film, he has been honored with festival
awards of the highest merit in San Francisco,
Chicago, New York, Washington, D.C.,
Columbus, in France, Belgium, Italy,
Scotland, Australia and Uruguay.

Photo by Harry Goldsholl

Note: Throughout this book trademarks and
brand names are pictured. The following lists
credit past owners at the time design was
accepted and current users as well as I can
remember or research.

Kleenex Brand Tissues® Kimberly Clark Corporation
ACCO® ACCO International, Inc.
Ultratones® Martin Senour Paints
Brach's® E.J. Brach & Sons, Inc.
Hi-C® Coca Cola Foods
Country Colors® Illinois Bronze
Perfection® Perfection American Gear Co.
Morningstar Farms® Miles Laboratories
Vienna Beef® Vienna Sausage Mfg. Co.
Pie Piper® Pie Piper Products
Brunswick® Brunswick Corporation
Ameritech® American Information Technologies
Ditto® Ditto, Inc.
Bauer & Black® Becton Dickson & Co.
Graham™ Graham Plating Company
Inland Steel Containers®
Stokely Van Camp®
Invequest™ Invequest, Inc.
Motorola® Motorola, Inc.
IMC® International Minerals & Chemicals
Baxter® Baxter Travenol Corporation
7UP® Seven-Up Story
Foulds® Foulds, Inc.
Aid Association for Lutherans®
GATX® General American Transportation Corp.
Quaker® Quaker Oats Company
Texoprint® Kimberly Clark Corporation

Japan, as the youngest son of a Japanese naval officer. Yoshi's boyhood dream of being a fighter pilot was shot down by Japan's defeat in the Pacific War. At the same time, however, he was introduced to American culture. Such country music greats as the late Hank Williams, Sr. inspired him in an early musical career and also helped him reconcile his differences with America. He realized that people are basically the same the whole world over and that fear and misunderstanding between the two nations had caused the war.

Other early aspirations of designing airplanes never materialized because Japan was forbidden to manufacture its own aircraft. In a more creative vein Yoshi directed his energies to what he considered the next best thing, graphic design.

Unsatisfied with his art education and years of design jobs in Japan, Yoshi came to the United States in 1964 and finished up his post graduate work at the Art Institute of Chicago. Before opening his own studio in 1976, Yoshi worked at a variety of jobs in both publishing and advertising. As Art Director of Cahners Publishing Co. (publisher of more than 50 business magazines), Yoshi had the opportunity to experience many of the critical aspects of graphic design. Later work for Playboy Enterprises helped him to get established enough to finally set up his own studio.

Yoshi's personal philosophy can be summed up in the following statement: "The goal of good design should be more than graphic problem-solving, and it should encompass all aspects of the communication process." To achieve this goal Yoshi works with a variety of visual elements including illustration, photography, typography, and graphics. Yoshi's ultimate goal is to be able to express himself equally well in any media. Design awards from such organizations as the Jesse H. Neal Editorial Achievement Committee, Communications Arts Magazine, New York Art Directors Club, Society of Publication Designers, Type Directors Club, and the Artist Guild of Chicago all attest to success.

He is married to Yoshiko Sekiguchi who helps him with many of his projects. Risa, the eldest of his three daughters, is an artist in her own right and is married to another artist, Kirk. Both have shown their works in galleries in the United States and Japan. Chika, the middle child, is currently studying graphic design at the University of Illinois at Urbana and is at Oxford, England, as an exchange student for a year. The youngest daughter, Juri, is in high school and participates in many school activities including the soccer and tennis teams.

Yoshi's future plans include concentrating on logo design and corporate communications. He's also working on a series of unique publications, focusing on the design of light airplanes, sports cars and helicopters. He would also like to spend more time studying ways to achieve peace in the truest sense. Said Yoshi, "I have been learning all these years. Now I think it's about time I applied them to a good cause."

72

Photo by Larry S. Brooks/Yoshiko Sekiguchi

Note: Many graphic elements throughout this book were permitted by each copyright owner for quotative use. I would like to thank them, and list their names in sequence for their proper credit.

U.S. Peace Institute
Nebraska Air National Guard
First Pacific Bank, Dai-ichi Kangyo Bank
Banque Nationale de Paris
Automobile magazine, a Murdoch publication
Standard Rate & Data Service, Inc.
VIP magazine, Playboy Clubs International
Playboy magazine, Japanese edition, Shueisha
Arakawa Chemical (USA) Inc.
Royal Co., Royal Host, Becker's
Illinois CPA Society
American Academy of Orthopedic Surgeons
United States League of Savings Institutions
Mercedes-Benz
Firestone Tire Co.
Plymouth Traveler, Chrysler Corp.
Gas Research Institute
Hewlett Packard
CNA Insurance
AT&T
Midwest Buddhist Temple
Nobart, Inc.
Jewish Community Centers of Chicago
Ideal
Institutions magazine, a Medalist publication
Building Supply News, a Cahners publication
Ceramic Industry, a Cahners publication
Brick & Clay Record, a Cahners publication
Professional Builder, a Cahners publication
Home Center magazine, a Vance publication
Wood & Wood Products, a Vance publication
Paper Trade Journal, a Vance publication
Plumbing Engineer, a Construction Industry Press publication
Domestic Engineering, a Construction Industry Press, publication
HVAC Products News, a Construction Industry Press publication
Rock Products, a Maclean Hunter publication
SCORE, Surgicot, Inc.
Supervisor Nurse, S-N Publications
American Heart Association
McDonald's
Nestlē
Art Director's Index, Adweek
Advertising Age
Nissan

1

2

BICYCLES AS NEW MEDIA

My nephew, Teppei, is a very interesting guy. After graduating from a famous university, he didn't follow the footsteps of his peers who went to work for big corporations. Instead, he has held many different jobs, such as managing a Japanese-style chain of pubs, promoting real estate, etc. In a way, he may have inherited my fickleness.

His latest venture was, strangely enough, selling cookies from bicycles shaped like spaceships. One day in Japan he saw television coverage of this bizarre franchise

business in New York, and bought the rights to do it in Japan.

Incidentally, I was in Japan in December, 1984, and he showed me the videotape of the New York cookie venture. Right then I concluded that it would be a failure, unless he could generate income from something besides cookies.

Teppei ignored my doubts and went on with the idea. It was a hit for the topic-hungry Japanese media and Teppei enjoyed the tremendous coverage. But, as I had predicted, the balance sheet didn't look good. Teppei kept trying and he eventually succeeded by

using the bicycle as an advertising media. Philip Morris used his service to distribute cigarette samples on the street. The promotion was a hit and soon other companies started using his service.

I designed many items for Teppei's venture, sort of a simple corporate identity program. One of them was a new design for the bicycle, much different than the New York model.

My design has two storage tanks on both sides of each wheel. It has a low center of gravity and the fuselages have flat planes for increased storage space as well as surface space for promotional use.

71

3

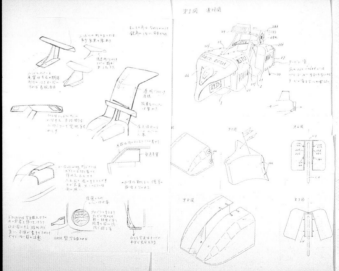

6

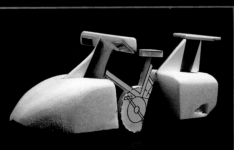

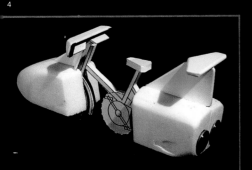

4

1 Shuttle Cycle (its official name) is tried by a curious boy at a campaign for Nissan.

2 Philip Morris used this media for sales promotion, giving away sample cigarettes. It was a smash hit.

3 Original bicycle design by New York franchiser. Note all the weight is over the wheels, which makes it very unstable.

4-5 Conceptual model I made out of styrofoam. Note storage tank is placed on both sides of each wheel.

6 Sketches in detail and plans for design patent application.

7 Obvious merit of these cycles is that they can go where motorized vehicles are prohibited.

CREATING SYMBOLS

As I mentioned before, I try to use a minimal amount of elements when I create logos and symbols. Just like a sauce thickens by simmering, I push the ''less is more'' theory to the point that the elimination of one element makes the design impossible to be understood.

First, I sketch elements to visualize the organization and combine them to make a logical shape. Sometimes I hang them on a wall, and stare at them from time to time for a week or so. Eventually, faults surface this way.

People have asked me how long it took to design a particular symbol. It is hard to say. Some of the best designs were created within a few minutes while some took as long as a month. Creativity cannot be measured in terms of time.

1 Radio station nicknamed ''Country Sunshine.''
2 Math Igler's Chicago Cabaret.
3 Ivory Isle Travel specializes in exotic trips to Africa.
4 Symbol for extracting electricity from gas.
5 Association of parents with missing children.
6 P Company, which sells cookies on bicycles.
7 Logo for Oak Park Symphony Orchestra.
8 Deer Creek racquet club.
9 Courts on 22. The 22 represents a road in Chicago's north suburbs.
0 Foreign Correspondents Club in Tokyo.
1 Land of Lincoln, with Abe's face.
2 Planning Graphics, a land surveying company.
3 The Stick and Rudder Flying Club, Waukegan, IL.
4 Symbol for a company that promotes self-motivation.

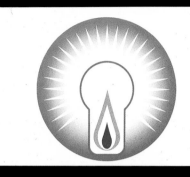

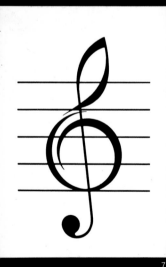

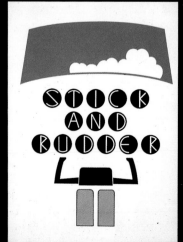